MCR

DEC 2 8 2018

D1266153

CULTURES OF THE WORLD

Yemen

Cavendish Square
New York

Published in 2019 by Cavendish Square Publishing, LLC
243 5th Avenue, Suite 136, New York, NY 10016

Copyright © 2019 by Cavendish Square Publishing, LLC

Third Edition

No part of this publication may be reproduced, stored in a retrieval system, or transmitted in any form or by any means—electronic, mechanical, photocopying, recording, or otherwise—without the prior permission of the copyright owner. Request for permission should be addressed to Permissions, Cavendish Square Publishing, 243 5th Avenue, Suite 136, New York, NY 10016. Tel (877) 980-4450; fax (877) 980-4454.

Website: cavendishsq.com

This publication represents the opinions and views of the author based on his or her personal experience, knowledge, and research. The information in this book serves as a general guide only. The author and publisher have used their best efforts in preparing this book and disclaim liability rising directly or indirectly from the use and application of this book.

All websites were available and accurate when this book was sent to press.

Library of Congress Cataloging-in-Publication Data

Names: Hestler, Anna, author. | Robinson, Peg, author. | Spilling, Jo-Ann, author.
Title: Yemen / Peg Robinson, Anna Hestler, and Jo-Ann Spilling.
Description: 3rd edition. | New York, NY : Cavendish Square Publishing, 2019. |
Series: Cultures of the world | Audience: 6+.
Identifiers: LCCN 2018031283 (print) | LCCN 2018032283 (ebook) |
ISBN 9781502641632 (ebook) | ISBN 9781502641625 (library bound)
Subjects: LCSH: Yemen (Republic)--History--Juvenile literature. |
Yemen (Republic)--Civilization--Juvenile literature. |
Yemen (Republic)--Social life and customs--Juvenile literature.
Classification: LCC DS247.Y48 (ebook) | LCC DS247.Y48 H46 2019 (print) |
DDC 953.3--dc23
LC record available at https://lccn.loc.gov/2018031283

Editorial Director: David McNamara
Editor: Elizabeth Schmermund
Copy Editor: Nathan Heidelberger
Associate Art Director: Alan Sliwinski
Designer: Jessica Nevins
Production Coordinator: Karol Szymczuk
Photo Research: J8 Media

The photographs in this book are used by permission and through the courtesy of: Cover Nick Ledger/Alamy Stock Photo; p. 1 Homo Cosmicos/Shutterstock.com; p. 3 Naeblys/Shutterstock.com; p. 5, 15 Naeblys/Shutterstock.com; p. 6 Samuel Colman/Bristol Museum and Art Gallery, UK/Bridgeman Images; p. 8 Sebastiano Tomada/Getty Images/ Reportage; p. 10 Peter Hermes Furian/Shutterstock.com; p. 12 Roel Slootweg/Shutterstock.com; p. 13 Peter Fitzgerald/Wikimedia Commons/File:Yemen regions map.png/CC BY 3.0; p. 14, 18 Oleg Znamenskiy/Shutterstock.com; p. 17 Jacques Descloitres/NASA/Getty Images; p. 19 (top, bottom) Vickey Chauhan/Shutterstock.com, Reptiles4all/Shutterstock.com; p. 20 Raju Soni/Shutterstock.com; p. 21 Yoshio Tomii/The Image Bank/Getty Images; p.22 Arthur Simoes/Shutterstock.com; p. 23 Kelly Cheng/Moment/Getty Images; p. 24 VCG Wilson/Corbis/Getty Images; p. 27 Picturenow/UIG/Getty Images; p. 28 Anton Ivanov/Shutterstock.com; p. 29 Culture Club/Getty Images; p. 30 Buyenlarge/Getty Images; p. 31 Antiqua Print Gallery/Alamy Stock Photo; p. 32 Bettmann/Getty Images; p. 33 Keystone Pictures USA/Alamy Stock Photo; p. 34 HandmadePictures/Shutterstock.com; p. 35, 38, 47, 63, 76, 84, 87, 119, 125, 126, 128 Mohammad Huwais/AFP/Getty Images; p. 36 Gamal Norman/AFP/Getty Images; p. 40 Natanael Ginting/Shutterstock.com; p. 42 Laurent Van der Stockt/Gamma-Rapho/Getty Images; p. 44, 46, 104 Khaled Fazaa/AFP/Getty Images; p. 45 Khalil Mazraawi/AFP/Getty Images; p. 50 Saleh Al-Obeidi/AFP/Getty Images; p. 52, 124 AFP/Getty Images; p. 54 Loose Grip 99/Wikimedia Commons/File:Yemen Sana'a Qat fields 1993 16788917612ce872e90 o.jpg/Public Domain; p. 56 DeAgostini/Getty Images; p. 60 Dea/V. Giannella/DeAgostini/Getty Images; p. 64, 99 Mohammed Hamoud/Getty Images; p. 66, 79 Anton Ivanov/Shutterstock.com; p. 68 George Steinmetz/Getty Images; p. 69 Maksim Dubinsky/Shutterstock.com; p. 70, 102 Eric Lafforgue/ArabianEye/Getty Images; p. 72 Dinosmichail/Shutterstock.com; p. 73 Danita Delimont/Gallo Images/Getty Images; p. 74 Ugurhan/iStock/Getty Images; p. 78 Khalid Alkainaey/Moment Open/Getty Images; p. 80 Richard T. Nowitz/Corbis/Getty Images; p. 81 Oleg Znamenskiy/Shutterstock.com; p. 82, 83 Essa Ahmed/AFP/Getty Images; p. 88 Muhammad Mahdi Karim at English Wikipedia/Wikimedia Commons/File:Kaaba Mirror like.jpg/CC BY SA 3.0; p. 90 https://pixabay.com/en/users/GLady-768/Wikimedia Commons/File:Aerial view of hajj party on mountain bluff approaching Mecca, Saudi Arabia.jpg/Public Domain; p. 91 Rod Waddington/Wikimedia Commons/File:Old Mosque, Yemen (14920736524).jpg/CC BY SA 2.0; p. 92 Adel Al-Sharee/Anadolu Agency/Getty Images; p. 94 Eric Lafforgue/Art In All Of Us/Corbis/Getty Images; p. 96 Ivrienen/Wikimedia Commons/File:Arabic clock in the metro of Cairo.jpg/CC BY 3.0; p. 97 Javarman/Shutterstock.com; p. 100 Hani Al-Ansi/Picture Alliance/Getty Images; p. 106 DMStudio/Shutterstock.com; p. 108 Yaser Alamoudi/Shutterstock.com; p. 110 Chris Mellor/Lonely Planet Images; p. 112 William Vanderson/Fox Photos/Getty Images; p. 115 Ferdinand Reus/Moment/Getty Images; p. 122 Roel Slootweg/Shutterstock.com; p. 130, 131 Wong Yu Liang/Shutterstock.com.

Printed in the United States of America

CONTENTS

YEMEN TODAY

YEMEN IS AN OLD LAND, WITH A HISTORY STRETCHING BACK TO the millennia before Judaism arose, before Christianity arrived, and before Islam came to dominate. Yemen incorporates the cultures and people of Asia, the Middle East, and Africa. Primarily Arab in ethnicity, Yemen nonetheless blends cultures and demographics from around the hub of the Middle East. The ancient roots of the country remain, clinging tenaciously, refusing to die out, in spite of famine, drought, illness, and war. Yemen's people live in apocalyptic conditions, but their culture and their soul remain.

Positioned at the southwestern tip of the Arabian Peninsula, Yemen, once part of the primary trade routes of history, has become increasingly isolated. Yet it is still within reach of much of Africa, Europe, Asia, and the Steppes.

Yemen is the land once known as Sheba—the land of the Queen of Sheba, Solomon's most famous wife. It was once a land of wealth and fame. It is blessed with natural beauty, with over 1,180 miles (1,900 kilometers) of coastline, stark deserts, and valley pasturelands.

Samuel Coleman's
interpretation of
the visit of the
Queen of Sheba to
Solomon (1830).

But Yemen is also a nation trapped in an ongoing rebellion. It is the poorest country in the Middle East. Anything one writes about the nation of Yemen has to arrive at these points. Yemen's violence and poverty overwhelm almost everything else to the outsider. War and poverty drive its violent ongoing rebellion, ensure the lack of effective intervention, color the lives of its people, and overshadow the hope of its future. Those who visit Yemen must be prepared to deal with the effects of rebellion and poverty on virtually all aspects of life. Those who do business in Yemen do business in a country shaped by desperate need.

Not long ago, Yemen, after many years of struggle, appeared to have stabilized its affairs. President Ali Abdullah Saleh had been reelected in 2006 and had been sworn in. Loans had been granted from multiple sources to allow the nation to develop its infrastructure and expand its place in the realm of international trade and manufacturing. Long-term investments were being made in the nation. The country had begun to look like a promising place in which to do business. Those reporting on Yemen at the time held out great hopes.

Those hopes were dashed during the slow collapse into chaos over the years between 2011 and 2014. During that period, referred to as the Arab Spring, much of the Arab world fell into turmoil as public outcry for increased representation in government grew. This was achieved in some countries, like Tunisia, while others, like Syria and Yemen, face continued conflict. In Yemen, President Saleh's rule was challenged and Shia factionalists occupied the capital. Since 2014, the situation has only worsened. At the time of this writing, Yemen is no longer considered one of the more promising states to emerge from the recent past. Instead, it faces one of the worst humanitarian crises in the world.

Yemen is an oil-producing country, but it is not a member of the Organization of the Petroleum Exporting Countries (OPEC). Unlike many Middle Eastern nations, its oil and gas production are largely in the hands of foreign investors, benefiting the oil companies more than the nation. Its reserves are declining, and its income from mined oil dropped in 2018 to roughly 25 percent of the gross domestic product (GDP). It has limited agricultural options, failing fishing stock, and no major manufacturing. Its economy is in desperate condition. Years of rebellion and disease have taken a toll on both Yemen's people and its infrastructure. Political turmoil ensures that it is not generally seen as a safe and desirable tourist destination. Until political stability is accomplished, it seems unlikely there will be any improvement on this front.

During this period of turmoil, Yemen has proven to be a magnet for various Middle Eastern and Islamic factions. It is being ripped in two by conflicting Shia and Sunni powers, with other nations taking sides out of concern for

"The Yemen Republic is an exotic mix of mountains, deserts, frequently rebellious tribesmen and guns. Maybe 16 million of them are in circulation."
—Brian Barron, BBC journalist

Six years of civil war has devastated Yemen; this photo shows what the historic district of Sanaa looked like before the war and in 2015.

their own future. Saudi Arabia and Iran—run by Sunni and Shia governments, respectively—each fear Yemen aligning with their opposing sect.

Similarly, Yemen has drawn both Russia and the United States (along with much of Europe and the Middle East) into its conflict. For these nations, the concern is the ability to continue to maintain connections and controls in such a volatile region, with oil and trade rights on the line. It's a matter of prestige, of global placement, and of perceived power. The violence in Yemen, which could spread throughout the region, presents a serious challenge to ongoing diplomatic, military, and commercial concerns, and places multiple ventures at risk.

Because of its current instability and its placement on the Arabian Peninsula, Yemen is a nation of international importance. Its rebellion—including ties with various Islamic factions, the desperate flight of its refugees, the illness festering in refugee camps, and the destruction of Yemen's infrastructure—all have outsize effects on global issues. Yemen, once one of the jewels of the Middle East, remains globally important today for the threat it poses to world security and peace.

Yet even in the face of all this, Yemen retains older, more constant features. The land—beautiful, arid, and agriculturally limited—remains. The Yemeni people remain, with their ancient cultures and their tribal traditions. The Yemeni cities remain, with their gingerbread-frosted houses decorated with white calligraphy citing scripture. Yemeni music and poetry remain, as do food and weddings, parties, and women drinking tea in the upper stories of tower houses. There are still tribesmen in white tunics, with culturally mandatory daggers tucked into the sashes bound over their stomachs. The Bedouin still travel the old trade routes, their camels swaying along old, old trails. The oud is still played. The standards of hospitality and generosity are still upheld. Yemen remains ... and Yemen is a nation worth knowing.

AMMAN

RDAN

IRAQ

IR

KUWAIT
KUWAIT
CITY

BAHRAIN
MANAMA
QATAR
DOHA

RIYADH

ABU
DHABI

UNITED ARAB
EMIRATES

GEOGRAPHY

SAUDI ARABIA

TREA

MARA

YEMEN

SANAA

**Yemen is located just south of Saudi Arabia
and north of the Gulf of Aden.**

THIOPIA

DJIB.

1

YEMEN OCCUPIES THE southwestern corner of the Arabian Peninsula. Its western shore is bounded by the Red Sea; its southern shore is bounded by the Gulf of Aden. The nation of Oman borders it to the east, and Saudi Arabia is its northern neighbor. Historically it has always been in contact with trade shipping down the Red Sea and out into the Arabian Sea.

"Don't worry about Yemen. Yemen started in peace, and it will end its revolution in peace, and it will start its new civil state with peace." —Tawakkol Karman, journalist and human rights activist

Yemen also lies southeast of Mecca, the holy city in Islam. Some people believe that Yemen's Arabic name, al-Yaman, means "southward (of Mecca)." Others argue that the word simply means "south," describing Yemen's position as the southernmost region on the Arabian Peninsula. The southern shores meet the waters of the Gulf of Aden, offering a point of access to the Arabian Sea and the Indian Ocean. The straits of Bab al-Mandab (Gate of Lament) lie to the west, opening into the Red Sea. The Suez Canal, at the head of the Red Sea, provides access to the Mediterranean Sea and the Atlantic Ocean far beyond. The port of Jiddah, in Saudi Arabia, is also situated on the Red Sea. The African countries of Eritrea and Djibouti lie across the straits from Yemen.

This system of waterways has served as part of the trade routes around Yemen through most of its history. The routes led both west and

Baobob trees grow across the rocky landscape of Socotra.

east, though until the building of the Suez, the final stage of transportation of goods and persons was overland before reaching the Mediterranean.

Yemen is a small country—about 203,850 square miles (527,970 square kilometers) in area, more than twice the size of Wyoming. Yemen's territory includes some islands in the Arabian Sea. Socotra, which lies about 560 miles (900 km) east of Aden, is the largest. Kamaran and the Hanish Islands in the Red Sea, and Perim Island in Bab al-Mandab are all smaller.

THE LAND

"A monkey in its mother's eye is like a gazelle."
—Yemeni proverb

People often think of Yemen as yet another desert country. However, in addition to the rich sands of the great Arabian Desert, the Yemeni landscape has features unusual for the Arabian Peninsula. It is blessed with beautiful coasts and sculpted peaks punctuated by valleys. The mountains of Yemen ensure the country gets more precipitation in the shadow of the hills than many other countries in the region. There are no lakes or rivers, but dry riverbeds called

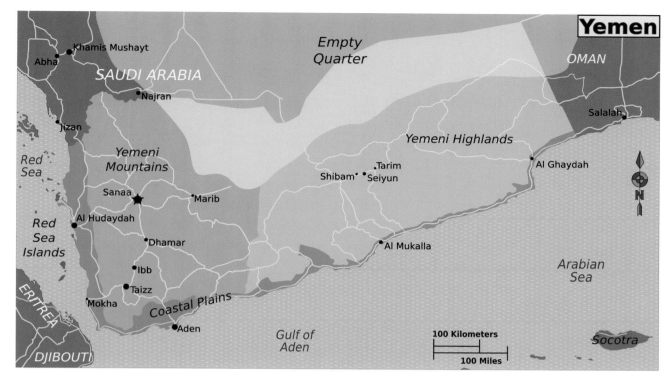

wadis fill with seasonal rains. These differences have contributed to regional variations in culture that have evolved over thousands of years.

Yemen can be divided into five regions. On the mainland are the four primary regions: the coast (Tihama), the mountains, the Eastern Plateau, and the desert. The islands can be defined as the fifth region, entirely separate from mainland Yemen

THE TIHAMA The Tihama, which means "Hot Earth," is a flat, narrow plain running parallel to the Red Sea. Across the water lies the East African shore, as little as 20 miles (32 km) away. Cultural exchanges between the people of the Tihama and their African neighbors, combined with a shared climate and environment, have led to some similarities on both sides of the sea. For example, reed huts can be found in both areas.

The sandy plain of the Tihama is 19 to 37 miles (30 to 60 km) wide. Irrigation has made parts of the plain fertile. The plain ends at rocky cliffs that are the edges of the Western Highlands. Over time, erosion of these cliffs has resulted

This map illustrates the five ecological regions of Yemen.

"Play the oud, miss,
with both right
and left hands,
Bring that fingertip
down and the
other up like this.
Sing the 'dan dan'
and then whatever
comes to your mind,
May God preserve
you and your
beauty increase,
I saw you when you
stood up, dancing,
the best among
the women."
—Yahya,
(d. circa 1705)

in the formation of deep wadis. The southern coastal plain is dotted with volcanic rocks and is the site of the important port of Aden. Over hundreds of years, Aden has acted as a doorway for trade and foreign influences.

THE MOUNTAINS Mountain chains known as the Western and Central Highlands form the backbone of the country. Geologically, the Arabian Peninsula was once part of the African continent. Millions of years ago, a rift between the two created the Western Highlands. These mountains are made of igneous rock—cooled lava—with stunning peaks that tower an average of 9,850 feet (3,000 meters) above sea level. Yemen's highest peak, Jabal al-Nabi Shuayb, at 12,028 feet (3,666 m), is also the tallest peak of the Arabian Peninsula. The Highland people, who live in thousands of villages perched on these craggy peaks, have historically been more isolated and more cut off from outside influences than people living along the coasts. The peaks of the Central Highlands are lower, at an average height of 3,280 feet (1,000 m).

Cradled within the mountainous regions lie the country's fertile plateaus, on which most of Yemen's urban centers, including the capital city, Sanaa, are located.

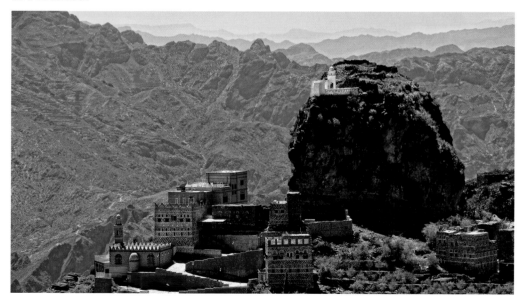

A highland Yemeni village sits on a mountaintop.

THE EASTERN PLATEAU AND THE DESERT The Eastern Plateau gradually merges with the vast sands of the Arabian Desert. The Rub al-Khali, which means "Empty Quarter," lies between Sanaa and Saudi Arabia.

There is little or no permanent settlement in the desert, but it is the home of nomadic herders known in Arabic as *bedu* (BEH-doo), or the Bedouin, who roam across the desert in search of grazing land for their cattle.

Between the desolate hills of the Eastern Plateau and the desert, and running along the southern coastline, lies the Wadi Hadramawt, a place well known for growing dates. Located on a limestone plateau, it is just high enough to catch sufficient rain to cultivate crops. This is one of the few areas in eastern Yemen fertile enough for cultivation.

A Yemeni tribesman crouches beside a wadi.

ISLANDS Yemen has about 112 islands, including Socotra, Kamaran, Perim, and the Hanish Islands. Each island has distinct climatic, geographic, and environmental characteristics.

The largest of the islands is Socotra, whose inhabitants are primarily Muslims of Arab, Somali, and South Asian origins. They speak Socotri, a Semitic language. The population is estimated at sixty thousand. The majority of the people are concentrated in the capital town of Hadibo and the western town of Qalansiya. Distant from mainland Yemen, Socotra is sometimes referred to as "the Galapagos of the Indian Ocean." Its unique ecosystem and its comparative safety from the violence of Yemen have led to increasing levels of ecotourism.

Due to the monsoon rains that occur from June to September, the islands have traditionally been isolated from the mainland. However, accessibility has improved since the opening of an airport in Socotra in July 1999.

As well as ecotourism, many people who live on the islands work in the fishing, livestock, and date-cultivation industries. The Yemeni government has been trying to attract investments to build up the tourism sector on many of the Yemeni islands.

SOCOTRA

Socotra, the "Island of Bliss," is the most famous of Yemen's islands. Mountainous and semiarid, it has an area of about 1,400 square miles (3,625 sq km). The people on Socotra are isolated from the outside world because monsoon winds make it difficult for planes or boats to reach them for four months. During this period, the islanders are self-sufficient. The island's economy was based on fishing and harvesting myrrh and aloe vera leaves, but it is increasingly dependent on ecotourism today.

Socotra is a botanist's dream. It has numerous rare plants, but many of them are threatened with extinction due to overgrazing. Some are renowned for their medicinal value, including the famous dragon's blood tree (Dracaena cinnabari), used in Asian medicine to cure eye and skin diseases. In the past, the Chinese also used it for dyes and cabinet lacquers, including cinnabar. Medieval European scribes used it to make ink.

WEATHER

As the most arable spot in the Arabian Peninsula, Yemen is often called "the green land of Arabia." After a successful rainy season, parts of Yemen look as though they are covered with a lush green carpet. The temperature varies with topography and elevation, but Yemen's mountains and location at the edge of the tropics largely determine its climate. However, over the past decades temperatures have risen and storms have increased, becoming especially damaging in Yemen's islands. Climate change has left Yemen with less and less reliable precipitation, and increasing water shortages.

Agriculture in Yemen depends on moist monsoon winds. When the winds blow from the south and southwest, the mountains trap the limited rainfall. During the rainy season, from April/May to July/August, the rains are very irregular, appearing as short, localized downpours. Torrential rains can wipe out a road in one village, while a neighboring village remains dry. The Wadi Hadramawt gets a sprinkling of rain.

The summer monsoons rarely reach the Empty Quarter. Sometimes this area receives little or no rain for years. Such unpredictable rains have challenged generations of farmers to build elaborate terraces and irrigation systems to trap the scanty rainfall.

Ibb, a province in the Western Highlands, is called the "fertile province" because it rains there every month. With water all year round, almost every type of crop can be grown there.

DUST STORMS

A shamal is a great dust storm that blows from the northwest across the Red Sea to the coastal areas of Yemen. It takes extremely high winds to create a dust storm. When the wind passes over areas of sparse vegetation, it picks up loose particles that can be as big as pieces of clay or as tiny as silt and fine sand. The particles are swept to great heights. Smaller ones can stay in the air for days. Some particles have even been found floating in the atmosphere above Alaska. Heavier grains of sand bounce along just a few inches above the ground.

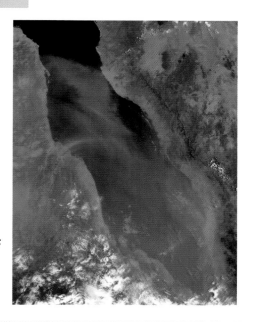

Sandstorms can be a real hazard. The particles act like sandpaper: they scrape away rock surfaces and remove paint from trucks. Dust storms can also erode valuable soil and destroy young crops.

Yemen's climate varies considerably. The Western and Central Highlands are drier and cooler than the rest of the country. It has been said that the air in those regions is "as temperate and sweet as the fresh spring." The winter season, from December to February, can get chilly, though, with temperatures sometimes dropping below freezing. Cozy sheepskin jackets keep the highlanders warm during the winter.

Along the Red Sea and the southern coast, the climate is hot and humid. Temperatures can rise to 104 degrees Fahrenheit (40 degrees Celsius) during June and July. To stay cool, people along the coast wear very loose clothes.

The desert and the Eastern Plateau are blisteringly hot. During the day, the temperature rises to 122°F (50°C), but it drops as soon as the sun sets.

PLANTS

Yemen's plants are fascinating and often exceptionally beautiful. In the Western Highlands, there are flowering bushes of tamarisk, ficus, and acacia. The tiny

Throughout history, the date palm has played a vital role in the Middle East. It grows in areas where there is little water because it has long roots that can tap water sources far below the surface. In Yemen, it flourishes around oases and in the Wadi Hadramawt. These trees can grow as tall as 92 feet (28 m). They start to bear fruit after four or five years and have been known to remain productive for up to 150 years. Each tree produces more than one thousand dates in a single bunch.

Dates are rich in iron and other minerals, protein, fat, and vitamins. The date palm also has many other uses: the trunks provide timber, the leaf ribs are used to make crates and furniture, and the smaller leaves are woven into beautiful baskets.

yellow and white flowers of the acacia are often used for dyes. Fruit-bearing trees such as mango and papaya, as well as Yemen's famous coffee shrubs, also grow well here.

The Central Highlands region has almond, peach, and apricot trees and a variety of grapevines that grow along its terraced slopes. Farther east, parts

The dragon's blood tree has been used for hundreds of years for medicinal purposes.

of the desert have no flora. Among the plants that have adapted to this arid region is the useful aloe; the dried juice of its leaves relieves sunburn.

ANIMALS

As recently as a century ago, Yemen had animals such as leopards, giraffes, pumas, oryx (large antelopes), and ibex (mountain goats). Sadly, the variety of wildlife has diminished because of desertification and hunting, as well as population growth, which has resulted in the clearing of many natural habitats to make way for buildings. Five mammal species and thirteen bird species are listed as threatened.

A Yemeni hyena on the hunt for prey

Among the animals native to the region are striped hyenas, caracals, hares, and foxes. One of the largest wild mammals still to be found in Yemen is the hamadryas baboon. Also called desert baboons, they travel together in groups.

Despite a general lack of animal wildlife, Yemen has plenty of birds: thirteen species are endemic to the country. More than four hundred species of migratory birds stop in Yemen on their way to Europe and Central Asia. In the Highlands, there are ravens and vultures. Farther east, weaverbirds build their nests on telephone poles.

Yemen also has a fair share of insects, spiders, and reptiles. Desert locusts live in areas where rainfall is erratic, but they travel en masse in search of food. Each year, swarms of desert locusts descend on farms. Within minutes, they devour vital crops. In the deserts and in some rocky parts of the highlands, scorpions dart around grabbing small prey such as lizards. Desert reptiles, such as the desert viper, bask in the torrid heat, maintaining their body temperature by absorbing the heat of their surroundings.

An alert Yemeni desert viper

Socotra has been called "the Galapagos of the Indian Ocean" because of its combination of intriguing and unique endemic species of flora and fauna, and its isolation from mainland species. These are excellent choices for academic study of evolution, and make Socotra a premier destination for those who want to experience a unique ecosystem. The island has been estimated as having over seven hundred unique endemic species of plants and animals, including the dramatic dragon's blood trees, whose sap is the source of cinnabar. The only endemic mammalian species is a bat; however, many other animal species are unique to the island. There are six endemic species of birds, including the Socotra warbler and the Socotra bunting. The island hosts over six hundred species of insects, of which an estimated 90 percent are endemic.

URBAN CENTERS

According to the CIA World Factbook, Yemen has a population of over twenty-eight million people, with much of the population living in rural parts of the country. The nation has thousands of small villages, while only about 37 percent of the population was based in cities as of 2018. The turmoil caused by the ongoing rebellion, with political unrest going back to 2011, has led to a massive flight of refuges, many deaths, and the extensive spread of contagious disease. Precise information regarding the finer points of the nation's population is difficult to pinpoint, and is in flux. The main cities of Yemen remain Sanaa, Aden, Taiz, and Hodeida. At the time of this writing, the city of Sanaa and the port of Hodeida are in the hands of Houthi rebel forces. Republic of Yemen forces and their allies have retaken 85 percent of the nation. Three-fourths of the population are considered to be in immediate need of relief and care—

twenty-two million Yemenis, of whom eight million have no source of food or any idea when they will have their next meal.

The old walled city of Sanaa was an architectural treasure prior to the most recent civil war.

SANAA Until the Houthi coup d'etat of 2014, Sanaa was the political capital of the Republic of Yemen. It is now held by Houthi rebels, and is considered the capital of the Sanaa governate, while the displaced president of the still-embattled regime of the Republic of Yemen maintains an alternate capital in Aden.

Sanaa is the largest, most important, and oldest city in Yemen. The name means "Fortified Place." At one time, the Sabeans, who ruled over one of Yemen's ancient kingdoms, used it as a highland fortress.

Aden is the best natural port in the Arabian Peninsula.

Sanaa is famous for its exquisite architecture and for the old walled center of the city. Many of the buildings in the medina are more than eight hundred years old. But Sanaa is also a contemporary metropolis. It is this blend of ancient and modern that makes the capital so fascinating.

Since 1960, its population has increased rapidly. Its population stands at approximately 2.8 million. Christians and Jews used to live in Sanaa, but today its residents are almost exclusively Muslim.

ADEN Aden (population 922,000), is the current capital of the embattled government of the Republic of Yemen. Built in the crater of an extinct volcano, it is surrounded by huge lava mountains that shield the port from the elements, making it the best natural port in the Arabian Peninsula. Throughout history, Aden has been crucial to trade and transportation between the East and West.

In 1839, Aden became a dependency of the British East India Company. Because its port lies equidistant from the important ports of Zanzibar, Bombay (now Mumbai), and the Suez Canal, Aden served as a coaling station for the British. Aden remained under British rule until 1967. After Yemen's unification in 1990, Aden was made the commercial capital and declared a free-trade zone.

As of 2018, Aden has suffered attacks from multiple factions of the rebellion, including Houthi loyalists and Saudi-backed rebels.

TAIZ Taiz (population 615,200), lies at the foot of Jabal Saber and sprawls over hills and lush green plains. The city has suffered an ongoing siege since 2015, continuing to the time of this writing in 2018. Before the Houthi coup in 2014, Taiz was a thriving commercial center. Its markets were well known for their female merchants, who were admired for their fierce bargaining skills. Taiz has been under constant conflict since then.

Taiz is a young city. Most of its concrete buildings were built after 1962, the year the Yemen Arab Republic (YAR) was established. Despite its new look, there are some old quarters in the city and many lovely mosques.

Taiz marketplace, circa 2009

HODEIDA (population 617,900) The port town of Hodeida is currently held by Houthi rebel forces. It is a critical resource, providing these forces with a major modernized shipping center. In 1961, a disastrous fire destroyed much of the city of Hodeida. The Soviets helped to rebuild and modernize the city, particularly its port, so that Soviet ships could make use of its facilities. The city continued to evolve, investing in concrete buildings and asphalt roads which replaced the reed huts of local fishermen. As such, it is a vital base for the Houthi faction.

As of 2009, the old Turkish quarter of the city remained intact, with handsome houses four stories high. The beautifully decorated doors of these houses were carved by Indian craftsmen who once accompanied traders to various ports. It is unknown what percentage of these old traditional beauties remain.

At the time of this writing, Hodeida was expected to come under attack by the forces of Saudia Arabia and the allied United Arab Emirates. Levels of fear for the outcome were high.

INTERNET LINKS

https://www.cnn.com/2018/06/11/middleeast/un-hodeidah-yemen -intl/index.html
This CNN article explores the attack on Hodeida that was expected at the time of this writing.

https://whc.unesco.org/en/list/385
UNESCO offers an overview of the old city of Sanaa.

HISTORY

Claude Lorrain's 1658 painting envisions the arrival of the Queen of Sheba to King Solomon's court.

2

I N THE LOCAL STORIES, THE LEGENDARY land that is now Yemen was once the location of Eden—now known as Aden. Cain and Abel died and were supposedly buried there. The glorious Queen of Sheba, who some claim was the beloved, "dark but beautiful" woman of the biblical Song of Solomon, ruled Yemen when it was known as "Saba." It was a rich land, the trading nation that dealt in frankincense and myrrh, in gold and spices. In Islamic legend, the descendants of Noah's son Shem moved away from Aden and all settled northwest of Yemen.

The history of Yemen is no less complex, if not quite as shining in splendor. The trade routes were real—the caravans and spices, as well as the ships sailing through the straits of Bab al-Mandab to the Gulf of Aden. The kingdom of Saba was real. And what of the Queen of Sheba? This is less certain, but probable: the Queen of Sheba casts a long shadow over Middle Eastern legend. So—where does it all begin?

"I rekindled the graveyard with my guitar, and broke open the shackles and coffins.

I yearn for my people with love, I restore them to life and erect buildings with poetry.

I compose eyes for the blind, and weave ears for the deaf."

—Muhammad Mahmoud al-Zubairi

The luxury and culture of the Arabian Peninsula came to Europe through folktales, legends, myths, and religious scriptures. Over time, Europe developed styles in literature, painting, architecture, and decoration intended to mimic Arabian culture. The resulting styles came to be known as "Arabesque."

BEFORE ISLAM

The earliest known civilization in southern Arabia began about 1000 BCE, when kingdoms based on five city-states flourished on the fringes of the eastern desert: Saba (also called Sheba), Qataban, Hadramawt, Awsan, and Main. Each of these kingdoms appears to have enjoyed periods of prosperity, and they often coexisted. They also shared a similar faith based on polytheism, or the worship of many gods. The legendary kingdom of Saba, which lasted for at least fourteen centuries, was probably the most powerful.

The kingdoms depended on agriculture and trade. Renowned for their brilliant building skills, the southern Arabians constructed ingenious dams and irrigation systems, enabling them to farm areas with little or no water.

Southern Arabia was the source of two precious resins: frankincense and myrrh. Frankincense was burned as an incense offering to the ancient gods, and myrrh was an ingredient in cosmetics, perfumes, and curative treatments. These aromatics were highly valued by the ancient Greeks, Romans, and Egyptians. Besides trading their own goods, Yemeni merchants sold ivory from Africa, spices and textiles from India, and fine silk from China.

Goods were shipped from India and China across the Indian Ocean to the port of Aden. From there, camel caravans transported them along the Incense Road to the markets of Egypt, the Mediterranean countries, and Mesopotamia. So many riches poured out of southern Arabia at that time that the Greeks and Romans called it Arabia Felix, which is Latin for "Happy Arabia."

THE FALL OF THE KINGDOMS

In the first century CE, when a Mediterranean seaman named Hippalus discovered a direct sea route between India and Egypt, the center of trade shifted westward to the coast of the Red Sea, where the kingdom of Himyar flourished. The caravan trails fell into disuse. This loss of trade to India precipitated the decline of Saba. Southern Arabia, including Yemen, became part of the Himyarite kingdom.

Around the same time, Christianity became the official religion of the Roman Empire. Demand for frankincense and myrrh plummeted, as the church

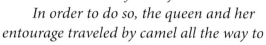

THE QUEEN OF SHEBA

The kingdom of Saba, or Sheba, is best known for its legendary queen. The story of the Queen of Sheba's visit to King Solomon appears in both the Old Testament and the Quran. In the story, a beautiful bird called a hoopoe brought news to King Solomon of the thriving kingdom of Saba and its queen. As queen of what may have been the most powerful kingdom in southern Arabia, she had great influence over the southern part of the Incense Road, while King Solomon controlled the northern end. Therefore, it was vital to cement friendly relations.

In order to do so, the queen and her entourage traveled by camel all the way to the court of King Solomon in ancient Palestine. On arrival, she presented the king with an abundance of gifts, including spices, gold, and precious stones. Her mission was so successful and the king so charmed that she became known as Queen of the Arabs.

associated their use with pagan rituals. The kingdoms of southern Arabia lost much of their wealth.

In 525 CE the king of Ethiopia seized Yemen. Forty-five years later, he attacked the kingdoms of Arabia but failed to conquer the region. He died soon after. After his death, the Himyarites enlisted the Persians' help to chase out the Ethiopians. When the Ethiopians were defeated in 575 CE, the Himyarite kingdoms came under Persian rule.

ISLAM

By the early seventh century CE, Islam had been introduced to the Arabian Peninsula by the Arab prophet Muhammad, born in 570 CE. The teachings

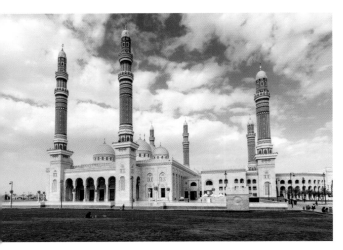

Al Saleh Mosque in
Sanaa, Yemen

of Muhammad spread rapidly, and the number of Islamic communities began to grow. By 628 CE, the Persian governor of Yemen had converted to Islam. Nearly everyone else in Yemen also converted.

After Muhammad died in 632 CE, centuries of conflict followed, and a number of Islamic dynasties came and went. Among these was the Zaidi Islamic sect, which established a state in northern Yemen in 897, when a descendant of the Prophet was invited to mediate a war between the Hashid and the Bakil tribes. Imam Yahya bin Husayn bin Qasim al-Rassi became the first political and religious ruler of the Zaidi dynasty. His teachings advocated an active political role for the imam, or religious leader. These principles laid the foundations of the Zaidi imamate, which held power in Yemen for more than one thousand years. The Sulayhids, whose rulers included the exceptional Queen Arwa, and the Rasulids, who excelled in the arts and sciences, were sects that subsequently came to power in the Middle Ages.

THE OTTOMAN EMPIRE I

In the early 1500s, the emerging powers of Europe became more interested in the lucrative trade between the Far East and the Mediterranean. Their attention became focused on controlling the Red Sea and Arabian coastal ports, which were vital arteries of the east—west trade. The Portuguese were the first to arrive. They annexed the island of Socotra in 1507. In 1513, Afonso de Albuquerque, who had conquered Goa in India, tried unsuccessfully to take the port of Aden. Spurred on by the Portuguese attempt, the Mameluke rulers of Egypt subsequently mounted a failed attack on Aden.

By 1517 the Ottoman Empire, centered in Turkey, had become the greatest military and naval power in the eastern Mediterranean and the Red Sea. To check Portuguese supremacy in the Indian Ocean, the Ottoman Turks arrived in Yemen. They conquered Taiz, Aden, and finally Sanaa in 1548.

During the Ottoman occupation, trade with Europe grew, and a great interest developed in the precious coffee beans grown in Yemen's highlands. The port of Mocha on the Red Sea became a pivotal point in the world coffee trade, attracting the English and the Dutch, who set up factories there.

The local population resented the occupation. As early as 1590, the Zaidi imam Qasim the Great challenged the Turks. While that attempt failed, the armies that finally expelled the Turks in 1636 were drawn from northern tribesmen and led by Qasim's son, Muayyad Mohammed.

For more than two hundred years, the Zaidi state extended its realm—east to the Wadi Hadramawt and as far north as the coastal region of Asir in what is now Saudi Arabia. Centralized control fell apart when some groups began to claim independence. A turning point came when the sultan of Lahij, in the south, blocked Zaidi access to the port of Aden in 1728. The British had been scouring the coastline for a coaling station en route to India, and this proved to be a golden opportunity for them to increase their influence.

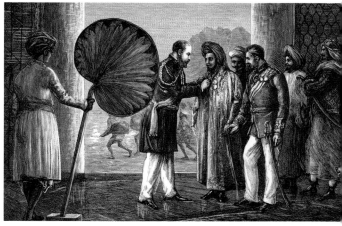

The Prince of Wales decorates the sultan of Lahij in 1875.

The British presence resulted in significant social changes. The number of Jewish, European, and Indian merchants in Aden increased. Indigenous Yemeni traders were drawn from the interior of the country to a new way of life. As a result, Aden grew into a metropolis with a cosmopolitan population.

THE BRITISH OCCUPATION OF SOUTH YEMEN

In the nineteenth century, a number of developments enabled Great Britain to expand its global realm. The development of the steam engine and railroads in the 1830s made transportation more efficient, and the ports of the Mediterranean and the Red Sea became connected to the ports of London and Liverpool in England. With the increasing activities of the British East India Company, Aden became an even more important port of call for ships and steamships on the route between Europe and India.

In 1839, the British took over Aden. It was ruled by the British East India Company until 1937, when it became a British crown colony. To protect Aden from a Turkish takeover, the British drew up a number of protection treaties with the local sheikhs, or tribal leaders. In return for British military protection, the sheikhs promised not to transfer their territory without British consent.

In this way, Great Britain's Protectorate of South Arabia was formed.

Under British rule, the port of Aden gained in size and importance. It benefited from political stability, improved commercial policies, and updated harbor facilities. Aden became a center for the shipment of goods and a hub of trading activity, surpassing the traditional ports of the Arabian and Red Sea coasts.

THE SECOND OCCUPATION

The British empire spread across much of the globe at its height.

In the mid-nineteenth century, the Ottoman Turks returned as a major influence in the Red Sea region. This led to a Turkish takeover of northern Yemen. The Ottomans reestablished their authority in the Tihama in 1849, forestalling British control of the Red Sea. The opening of the Suez Canal in 1869 prompted the Turks to expand into the highlands. They occupied the major cities, finally capturing the Zaidi capital of Sada in 1882.

Ottoman and British interests clashed. Both powers agreed to demarcate boundaries between them and drew a border between north and south in 1905. This sealed the division between North Yemen and South Yemen, a division that lasted until unification in 1990.

The local population opposed the Turkish occupation. There were a number of uprisings by the Zaidis as well as by the northern Tihama tribes under the leadership of Sayyid Mohammed al-Idrisi. In 1904, Imam Yahya ibn Mohammed organized a resistance movement among the highland Yemenis. Under the 1911 Treaty of Daan, he finally forced the Turks to accept a division of power granting him autonomy in the highlands.

After the Ottoman Empire's defeat in World War I in 1918, the Turks withdrew from North Yemen. The Treaty of Lausanne officially ended Turkish

rule. North Yemen obtained international recognition as an independent state ruled by the powerful Imam Yahya. South Yemen remained in the hands of the British.

A procession of ships flows through the Suez Canal upon its opening in 1869.

THE ZAIDI IMAMATE

After gaining independence, Imam Yahya set about consolidating central authority and securing the borders. In the Tihama in 1925, he conquered the Idrisi forces, who then allied themselves with Saudi Arabia. Yahya's northern advances alarmed the Saudis, culminating in the Saudi-Yemeni War of 1934.

President Abdullah Sallal negotiates with tribal leaders in 1964.

This ended with the Taif Treaty, leaving Asir and Najran temporarily under Saudi rule. These territories are still in dispute today.

Fearing that outside contact might result in challenges to his authority, Imam Yahya adopted a policy of isolation. Nevertheless, Yahya realized that to be secure, he needed foreign technology, particularly for the military. This required education and training. In the 1930s, the first Yemenis went abroad to be educated. Once exposed to foreign ideas, however, they began to question Imam Yahya's leadership. In 1948, a group of liberal reformers, led by Abdullah al-Wazzir, assassinated Imam Yahya, but Yahya's son, Imam Ahmad, drove them out. Later, Imam Ahmad established his own government, which closely resembled that of his father.

THE YEMEN ARAB REPUBLIC

Following Imam Ahmad's death in 1962, his son Muhammad al-Badr came to power. Within a week, a group of army officers staged a coup, deposed him, and proclaimed North Yemen to be the Yemen Arab Republic (YAR), with Colonel Abdullah Sallal as the president. Imam al-Badr fled to the northern mountains and organized forces to help him restore his regime. The country plunged into civil war. Egypt and the Soviet Union supported the republicans, while Saudi Arabia and Britain backed the imam's royalists.

By 1967, the fighting had reached an impasse. The royalists faced defeat, and internal conflict troubled the republican ranks. As a result, the Egyptians withdrew their troops, and Abdul Rahman al-Iryani replaced Sallal as president. The civil war finally ended in 1970 when Imam al-Badr was exiled to Britain. The republicans established a government that lasted until 1974, when a group of army leaders took control and steered the country in a conservative direction.

THE PEOPLE'S DEMOCRATIC REPUBLIC OF YEMEN

The 1960s were turbulent times for South Yemen as well. Around the same time that Imam al-Badr was overthrown, South Yemen underwent a socialist revolution.

Despite opposition in 1963, the British made Aden a crown colony included in its protectorate, the Federation of South Arabia. Although Britain promised to grant independence to the federation at a later date, nationalism had already swept through the south. A left-wing rebel movement known as the National Liberation Front (NLF) was organized and began a campaign of terror.

British Lord Shackleton (*left*) shakes hands with President Qahtan al-Shabi after the independence of South Yemen in 1967.

The Federation of South Arabia collapsed in 1967. The NLF declared South Yemen independent. In 1970, it became the People's Democratic Republic of Yemen (PDRY) under the leadership of President Qahtan al-Shabi. Eventually, the NLF developed into the Yemeni Socialist Party (YSP).

The economy of the new republic was in shambles. In the late 1960s, the country suffered from a long drought. The closure of the Suez Canal in 1967 aggravated the effects of the loss of British trade and investment and further reduced Aden's economic role in the world. These factors led to widespread hunger, economic hardship, social problems, and even deaths in many parts of the country. The PDRY managed to stay afloat only with financial aid from the Soviet Union and other communist countries of Eastern Europe.

Further, an internal ideological power struggle threatened the country's political stability. Political sentiment became more left-wing and even more closely allied with the communist bloc. In 1969, President al-Shabi was ousted in favor of President Salim Rubayi Ali, who brought most of the economy under government control.

UNIFICATION

At the beginning of the 1970s, both the YAR and the PDRY relied on foreign aid to revive their war-damaged economies. Saudi Arabia and Western Europe

The impact of the Suez Canal can't be understated. This artificial waterway, completed in 1869, solved a previously critical challenge to shipping and trade in the Eastern Hemisphere. The American equivalent, the Panama Canal, solved a similar problem in the Western Hemisphere. Without these two man-made passages, the only route from the Atlantic to the Indian Ocean, and from  *the Atlantic to the Pacific, involved long—and dangerous—trips around the southernmost tips of Africa (the Cape of Good Hope, shown above) and South America (Cape Horn). Shipping time was prolonged. The loss of ships, crews, passengers, and cargo was high.*

The Suez Canal altered trade systems around the globe. During times when it closed, such as the closure caused by Israeli-Arab conflict in 1967, there were shattering effects on communities dependent on the trade. Aden was badly damaged by the 1967 closure, with lasting effect on Yemen's fortunes.

supported the YAR, while the PDRY was aided by the Soviet Union. Strained relations resulted in a series of wars along their border.

In 1978, after a succession of leaders, Colonel Ali Abdullah Saleh became president of the YAR. He embraced a Western-style market economy. During the 1980s the economy grew stronger under his rule.

Meanwhile, in the PDRY, civil war broke out in 1986. Financial aid also dried up with the collapse of the Soviet Union. Bankrupt, the PDRY turned to its northern neighbor for help.

Previously there had been unification talks between the two Yemens, but the discovery of oil in the desert bordering both countries sped up the process. They finally merged on May 22, 1990. Saleh became president of the new nation. A southerner, Ali Salim al-Baydh, became vice president.

The first few years for the new nation were filled with trouble. A disagreement between supporters of the president and those of the vice president resulted in a civil war in 1994. But within a few months, troops supporting the president won the war, and the country remained united.

POST-UNIFICATION

Yemen enjoyed a short period of relative peace after the ascension of Saleh, although there were some incidents of tourist kidnappings and other acts of terrorism. The nation managed to establish a democratic system. Although the discovery of oil and the increase in oil prices in 2000 boosted the government's revenues, Yemen still remained one of the poorest countries in the Middle East. Further, it remained a land with a long and divisive history of conflict, not only with outsiders but between internal groups and varied religious contenders. By 2009, Yemen again showed signs of division, with a rising insurgency among a Shia Islamic faction known as the Houthis.

Yemenis take to the streets as part of the Arab Spring uprisings in 2011.

Islam is divided in large part between the Shia and Sunni sects, a division that dates back to the assassination of the prophet Muhammad's grandson, Husayn, in 680 CE. The schism, never simple, has evolved over the past millennium, becoming a complex matter not easily summarized. For outsiders, perhaps the most important considerations are which nations and regions are dominated by what sect, and whether there are ongoing alliances with Saudi Arabia or Iran.

Saudi Arabia is majority Sunni, ruled by Sunni leaders. Iran is majority Shia, ruled by Shia leadership. The nations are the two most important leaders in the Middle East, and they are in contention. Each seeks allies throughout the region, supporting groups that can promote their power through peaceful or violent means.

Yemeni security forces stand guard outside a government building in Sanaa in 2011, following widespread protests.

Under the rule of President Saleh, Yemen was orderly, but its government was corrupt, with extensive nepotism. Tensions built between 2009 and 2011, at which time the "Yemen Crisis" began, with the advent of the Arab Spring uprisings.

THE BREAKDOWN

Protests influenced by the Arab Spring began in January of 2011. On June 3, 2011, opposition to Saleh's rule led to a direct shelling of the Yemeni presidential palace and the palace mosque. President Saleh was injured; he was later transported to Saudi Arabia for medical treatment. He returned in September of 2011.

Fighting continued, with Houthi rebels and al-Qaeda both taking part in attacks. Ongoing pressure to remove Saleh from office led, at last, to his agreement on November 23, 2011, to transfer power to his vice president, Abdrabbuh Mansur Hadi. Hadi was formally elected on February 21, 2012, and sworn in on February 25.

The change in leadership failed to secure peace. On May 21, 2012, a suicide bomber killed more than one hundred and wounded more than two hundred at a rehearsal being held for a military parade in Sanaa, the capital city. On December 5, 2013, an attack was made on a Defense Ministry hospital, also in Sanaa. The attack involved a bombed vehicle used as a ram and armed attackers, and led to fifty-two dead.

On December 12, 2013, a mistaken US drone attack hit a wedding party. The death toll was fourteen, with more wounded. The resulting international outcry led to the cessation of officially sanctioned use of drones in attacks, with Yemen's parliament voting on December 15 to end all drone strikes.

Meanwhile, Houthi protests increased, virtually stopping normal day-to-day life in Sanaa. In July 2014, the Hadi government announced an increase in fuel prices in response to international pressure to end subsidies. This unpopular decision gave Houthi rebels the public support needed to increase their attacks on the government.

THE HOUTHI COUP D'ETAT

On September 21, 2014, the Houthi rebels, with the aid of Saleh loyalists, took control of Sanaa. Outright war soon began between the Houthis and the Hadi government, starting with the kidnapping of Hadi's chief of staff, Amed bin Mubarak on January 17, 2015. Mubarak was released after ten days. On January 20, 2015, Houthi forces occupied the Presidential Palace. In the aftermath, President Hadi and his cabinet resigned, and the Houthi forces offered to withdraw from Sanaa if requested changes were made to the Yemeni constitution. A UN report later concluded that former president Saleh had provided "direct support" to the rebels in the takeover.

No agreement was reached between the Houthis and the Hadi government, however. On February 11, 2015, both the United States and the United Kingdom (UK) withdrew from their respective embassies in Yemen. Later that month, President Hadi withdrew his resignation and fled to Aden. Amid ongoing violence, which included an attack claimed by the Islamic State of Iraq and Syria (ISIS), the Houthis expanded their territory, taking the international airport at Taiz.

A joint-Arab coalition led by Saudi Arabia sent warplanes to attack Houthi targets. This was a largely Sunni alliance, attempting to defeat the Houthis. Shia-dominated Iran backed the Houthis. Over the following months, violence continued, including the death of the governor of Aden in an ISIS-claimed car bombing.

On November 28, 2016, the Houthis officially formed a new government in Sanaa. Abdul Aziz Habtoor, a defector from Hadi's government, was reported as the leader of the new Houthi administration. In December 2017, Saleh declared

A Houthi rebel stands guard outside the destroyed Presidential Palace in Sanaa.

the withdrawal of his support for the Houthis and sided with his former enemies in the Hadi government. Later that month he was assassinated by Houthi forces during an attack near Sanaa.

Throughout 2017, violence continued throughout Yemen. Players involved included Saudi Arabia and its allied Sunni nations, Iran, the United States (newly engaged by President Donald Trump's commands after his swearing-in in 2017), the Muslim Brotherhood, al-Qaeda, ISIS, the Houthis, and more. The result has been referred to as a "chaos state" by the think tank Chatham House and others.

Out of this chaos has come famine and plague. As Médicins Sans Frontières reported in 2017, "The escalating fighting in Yemen has created a large-scale humanitarian emergency, with the war and blockade by the Saudi-led coalition taking a heavy toll on civilians. The collapse of the health system and the deterioration of living conditions have had a devastating effect on the population." In May 2017, reports came of a cholera outbreak that remains in progress at the time of this writing in 2018.

INTERNET LINKS

https://www.acleddata.com/2018/02/09/yemen-the-worlds-worst -humanitarian-crisis-enters-another-year
The Armed Conflict Location and Event Data Project (ACLEDP) website includes neutral reporting of facts regarding ongoing conflicts, including a summary of Yemen's war.

https://www.cnn.com/2013/07/10/world/meast/yemen-fast-facts /index.html
This site offers clear information about the progression of events in Yemen over the past decade.

https://fanack.com/yemen
This website is dedicated to providing factual information on the nations of the Middle East, on a country-by-country basis.

GOVERNMENT

The flag of Yemen flies in front of a government building in Sanaa.

"The master of
the people is
their servant."
—Yemeni proverb

3

Y EMEN IS CURRENTLY IN THE MIDST of a terrible civil war complicated by outside alliances and internal divisions. The government described below is still considered the official government ruling Yemen. However, it is uncertain to what degree the Republic of Yemen holds authority. It is even more uncertain what form of government will take over if and when fighting concludes. The various authorities attempting to hold sway in the interim must be considered provisional governments through occupation and, to a large extent, martial law.

As of the spring of 2018, there are three major factions controlling different territories of Yemen. The first is loyal to the displaced President Hadi. The second faction is the Houthis and their regional allies. The third is al-Qaeda.

THE REPUBLIC OF YEMEN

Yemen's political system is unique in the Arabian Peninsula. The Yemeni people wanted a democratic system of government based on direct popular elections, freedom of speech, and an independent judiciary. Their struggle for democracy came from the people's desire to end absolute rule.

CONSTITUTION

Before unification, the two Yemeni countries had different political systems. The YAR was a capitalist republic, ruled under a provisional constitution dating back to the 1970s. In contrast, the PDRY favored Marxist principles; government policy was determined by the Yemeni Socialist Party.

Once both Yemeni nations had agreed to unite, the legislatures of both the YAR and the PDRY then approved a draft constitution for the new nation. This constitution was a major deviation from the previous two. Despite opposition

Residents are evacuated from Yemen during the 1994 civil war, after which the nation's constitution was revised.

TRIBES AND ALLIANCES

In 2009, the Hashid and Bakil tribes were the most prominent in Yemen. Many tribesmen held important positions in the government, and a number of tribal sheikhs were unofficial government employees who received salaries and cars. The late former president Ali Abdullah Saleh was a member of a Hashid tribe near Sanaa. In the current state of national turmoil, however, Yemeni tribes' importance and influence depends on more immediate factors, including which allies and groups remain faithful friends, and which have changed sides during the war.

from certain factions, the majority supported the constitution in a popular referendum held in mid-May 1991. Yemen was governed by this constitution until October 1, 1994, when some amendments were made.

The revised constitution defines the Republic of Yemen as "an independent and sovereign Arab and Islamic country." It states that the republic "is an indivisible whole, and it is impermissible to concede any part of it. The Yemeni people are part of the Arab and Islamic nation." The revised constitution stipulates that sharia (Islamic law) is the source of all law. Sharia is an interpretation of the reading of the Quran, along with the sayings and actions of the prophet Muhammad. A further amendment abolished the five-member presidential council, which included the president and the vice president.

GOVERNMENTAL STRUCTURE

The constitution sets out a parliamentary system of government based on direct popular elections. Anyone who is over eighteen years of age can vote. The Assembly of Representatives serves as the legislative branch of the state. Yemen has a two-part, or mixed, legislature: a lower house called the House of Representatives and an upper house called the Shura Council. *Shura* is Arabic for "consultative." The president created the Shura Council in May 1997.

The lower house consists of 301 elected members who serve for six-year terms. The upper house is made up of 111 members who are appointed by the president. This two-part legislature in Yemen means that power was shared

Abdul Aziz Abdul
Ghani, the chairman
of Yemen's Shura
Council (right),
listens to the
Malyasian prime
minister Abdullah
Badawi in 2007.

between the two houses, and a concurrent majority must be achieved in order to pass any legislation. The Assembly of Representatives is responsible for enacting laws, approving policies and development plans, supervising public spending, and ratifying international treaties. The president cannot dissolve it, except in an emergency.

According to the constitution, the president and a cabinet of ministers make up the executive branch. The president is elected for a seven-year term. He is empowered to appoint the vice president, the prime minister, and other ministers on the advice of the prime minister.

Yemen is divided into twenty-two administrative units known as governorates, sometimes called provinces. Headed by governors, these governorates are divided into smaller units known as districts and local councils. The local government administers various aspects of community life, such as health, education, and tax collection.

Not everybody embraced the original constitution wholeheartedly. Among those who opposed it were religious groups in the north, including the Muslim Brotherhood. They objected strongly to the proposed constitution and urged the rest of the population to boycott it because it was not based exclusively on Islamic law.

The Muslim Brotherhood was founded in Egypt in 1928, and it has grown to be one of the largest and most influential Islamist groups in the world today. It preaches social justice and the eradication of poverty and corruption. The Muslim Brotherhood is particularly against colonialism by Western countries across the Middle East.

LAW

The principles of Islam concern all aspects of life, and Islam provides its followers with a means of ordering their daily lives according to the will of Allah (God). Muslims believe that God's words were revealed through the prophet Muhammad and later became the Quran, the holy book of Islam. This sacred text was supplemented by a collection of Muhammad's sayings known as the Hadith.

Together, they form the basis of sharia ("God's way"), which is an interpretation of the law of Islam. Sharia includes a range of rules governing behavior. These include religious rituals such as prayer, family matters such as marriage, and how a Muslim should behave in society.

The state and the judiciary are separate within Yemen's legal system. This means that judges can carry out their duties independently, and the courts have the power to decide all disputes and crimes. The law is the only authority that governs their work.

وإذا حكمتم بين الناس ان تحكموا بالعدل
صدق الله العظيم
العدل أساس الحكم

Yemenis charged with terrorist attacks face judges at a court in Sanaa in 2002.

The structure of the courts is consistent with the administrative divisions of the country. Every district has a court of first instance, which tries civil, criminal, matrimonial, and commercial cases. Every governorate has a court of appeal that looks into appeals against the decisions of the district courts. The Supreme Court, located in the capital city of Sanaa, is the highest court of appeal in the land. Headed by a president of the court with two deputies and nearly fifty judges beneath him, the Supreme Court looks into appeals against decisions of the courts of appeal.

CIVIL WAR

Following unification, more than forty new parties vied for popular support. The first election, held on April 27, 1993, drew enthusiastic voters. The result was a three-party coalition: the General People's Congress (GPC), formerly dominant in the north; the Yemeni Socialist Party (YSP), formerly dominant in

PRESIDENT SALEH

The late President Ali Abdullah Saleh was born in 1942 in the village of Bait al-Ahmar in the Sanaa governorate, where he attended a Quranic school for his elementary education. In 1958, he joined the armed forces, and to continue his studies, he enrolled in the noncommissioned officers' school in 1960.

President Saleh had a long and successful military career in which he was promoted through the ranks. The former president of North Yemen, he assumed office as president of the Republic of Yemen after unification in 1990. He died on December 2, 2017, at the hands of Houthi insurgents—and former allies.

the south; and the Yemeni Congregation for Reform, also known as the Islah Party, which represented tribal and Islamic interests.

Soon after the election, clouds began to gather. A disagreement over the sharing of power between the GPC, led by President Ali Abdullah Saleh, and the YSP, led by Ali Salim al-Baydh, pushed the country to the brink of disaster in 1993. A full-blown civil war broke out on May 4, 1994.

Shortly after the war began, al-Baydh proclaimed the independent Democratic Republic of Yemen, hoping to win the support of those countries on the Arabian Peninsula that did not support Saleh. However, Saleh's troops surrounded Aden. The secessionists, including al-Baydh, fled to other parts of the Arab world.

After the YSP's defeat, President Saleh affirmed his commitment to democracy. President Saleh won the 1999 election by an overwhelming majority, although there were angry opposition boycotts, claims of vote rigging, and violence at polling booths.

MAJOR POLITICAL PARTIES

At the time of the Houthi coup, the primary political party in Yemen was the General People's Congress (GPC), which held a practical if not an actual monopoly on power. The GPC seldom presented a strong platform, serving instead almost as a shura, *or an advisory and consulting body. In many cases, politicians running as independents will join the GPC later, the nature of the body making it a useful professional resource once in office.*

The primary opposition party is the Yemeni Congregation for Reform, also called Islah. It was founded to maintain a strong religious (Islamic) element in government, in the face of what were felt to be secular Marxist influences following Russia's involvement with Aden. The party has ties with the Muslim Brotherhood. The old Yemeni Socialist Party remains, providing a limited voice for those still faithful to the former government.

In February 2009, the Assembly of Representatives approved a two-year postponement of its legislative elections. This was an attempt to calm heightening tensions between the governing party and the opposition over the fairness of elections. The elections had been scheduled for April 2009, but they were shifted to April 2011—at which time the events of the Arab Spring triggered the lead-up to the Yemen Crisis. Faced with widespread protests, President Saleh announced in 2011 that he would serve out the remainder of his term and not seek reelection in the 2013 presidential elections. However, public anger at his abuses of power continued. Saleh was badly injured in an assassination attempt in June 2011, and stepped down in February 2012, passing the presidency to his deputy, Abdrabbuh Mansur Hadi. But this was not the end of Saleh's influence in Yemen. In 2016, he allied with Houthi rebels to overthrow President Hadi and Prime Minister Mohammed Basindawa. This alliance faltered in 2017, and Houthi rebels assassinated Saleh in December of that year.

It is hard to guess where Yemen will be when the civil war ends, or what kind of nation will rise from the current catastrophe of war, poverty, deprivation, and damage facing Yemen. The United States has chosen to back the Republic of Yemen and its displaced President Hadi, but it seems unlikely that a seamless, fluid return to the government and society of 2009 can occur. Even if and when the Republic of Yemen completely overthrows the Houthis, there remains al-Qaeda to be dealt with. There are also southerners who hope for a separatist government, dividing the nation again between North and South Yemen.

In the meantime, the destruction caused by the civil war has done untold damage to the nation's people and infrastructure. Thousands have fled as refugees; thousands more have been lost to combat, disease, famine, and drought. The great hope is that sometime in the foreseeable future the violence will end.

"Furthermore Yemen is a leading pioneer in democratic practice, lots of brothers and friends testified on that."
—Ali Abdullah Saleh

INTERNET LINKS

https://www.theatlantic.com/international/archive/2018/02/the -war-in-yemen-and-the-making-of-a-chaos-state/551987
This 2018 article from the *Atlantic* examines Yemen as a "chaos state."

https://www.bbc.com/news/world-middle-east-29319423
This concise BBC explainer examines the many players in the Yemen Crisis.

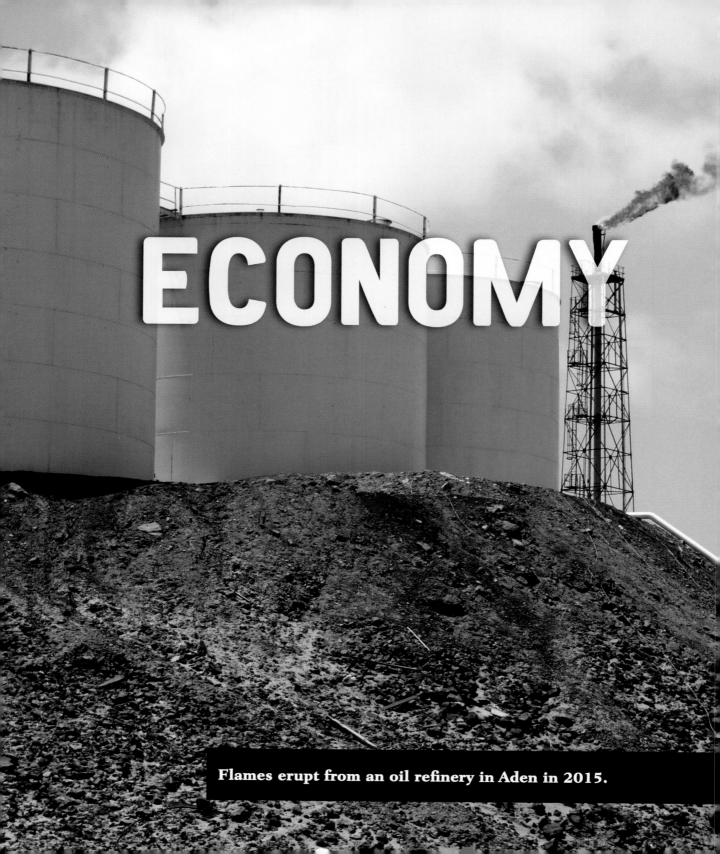

ECONOMY

Flames erupt from an oil refinery in Aden in 2015.

YEMEN IS SAID TO BE THE LAND THAT held Eden. Like most of the places humankind has settled over the millennia, Yemen offered land that could be farmed—although not much land compared to the Nile River valley and other "cradles" of civilization. And yet, in places like Ibb, where the hills lie just right and the rain clouds linger, Yemen offers an amazing array of gardens and farms, even more precious for the difficulty the arid land poses.

But Yemen's farmland has never been able to offer much beyond survival. Yemeni farms in the best of circumstances provide subsistence for the country and little more. For wealth, Yemenis have had to engage in trade. They've exported goods provided by the wild flora of their ecology, including qat, which are leaves from a shrub that are chewed for their stimulating effect, and coffee beans.

What was true in the past remains true in modern times. Throughout Yemen's modern period, it has depended on trade, and on exported labor. Trade has grown to include a limited oil and gas trade. Yemen's laborers are

4

"If you have honey, don't lick the pot clean."
—Yemeni proverb

South Yemeni fighters stand guard in 1957. South Yemen was a socialist people's republic, based on Marxist economic principles.

increasingly likely to train for an international job market dependent on technological skills. Yemen continues to farm what it can, and it trades or labors for what the land won't give.

In times of trouble, Yemen is forced to depend on strangers. Now, in the middle of a civil war so extreme that the United Nations (UN) has called it the worst humanitarian crisis of 2018, Yemen depends on its allies and on charities for help. Long before the civil war, Yemen depended on outside support—often in excess of what it could offer in return. Things are worse now only in the extremity of need.

THE CHALLENGE

Before unification there were two Yemens—North Yemen, a capitalist republic, and South Yemen, a socialist people's republic. Both North and South depended on support from neighbors.

With unification, Yemen inherited two opposing economic systems. After unification, the northern YAR system was adopted.

AGRICULTURE

In the period before the civil war, agriculture contributed around 9 percent of Yemen's gross domestic product (GDP). Much of its agricultural activities depend on rain, but the rains are temperamental, challenging farmers then and now to construct ingenious irrigation systems to catch the water. The highlands are covered with exquisite terraces that prevent fertile soil from being washed away. The Yemeni authorities invested in building dams and modern irrigation systems to increase the availability of water for agricultural use. Many of these have been lost to fighting, as opposing forces attempt to deprive each other of resources that could be useful in the war.

A DESPERATE SITUATION

In 2014, with its economy already threatening to collapse, Yemen attempted to shore up its flailing economy by taking $570 million in extended credit from the International Money Fund (IMF) on condition of attempting major economic reform and revitalization. While the nation operated in good faith, the Houthi coup and the following civil war has ensured that there is no reliable hope of fulfilling the obligations to repair the economy.

As a result, Yemen is in worse condition than previously, with fewer options open. The nation's GDP as of 2017 was a mere $68.95 billion, and it had been falling for the two years previous. The GDP per capita was $2,300 as of 2017.

Although the society is becoming less agrarian, agriculture is still the primary occupation of more than three-quarters of the population. Households farm small plots of land that produce very little. Each year, fewer people farm and less food is produced. Each year, crops are reduced.

Once self-sufficient in food, Yemen is dependent on international trade imports. Working for wages abroad or in the cities has become an attractive alternative to working in the fields. This has reduced the labor force. On the other hand, the resulting remittance income sent back to Yemen by foreign workers helps to diversify the economy. That diversity has been once more robbed through war, though. Formerly, when workers returned to their villages, some of them had saved enough money to open shops or businesses.

Another reason food imports are needed is that more qat, a shrub whose leaves are chewed for their stimulating effect, is being grown as a cash crop at the expense of food crops. Because of high local demand, many farmers have converted their land to qat fields. The growing of qat is controversial because Yemen is a poor country, yet half of its arable land is used to grow this drug. Qat is addictive, and its use has been linked to long-term health issues.

Although women chew qat, its use is more prevalent among men. Many families spend a large portion of their income on qat and a fair amount of their time chewing it. This habit used to be confined to the rich elite, but it became affordable to the rest of society when incomes rose. It is claimed

Qat fields extend across the rural landscape outside of Sanaa.

that up to 90 percent of the population uses this drug for up to five hours a day.

Nonetheless, Yemen's agricultural output remained quite varied before the war. Its grains included sorghum, corn, wheat, barley, and millet. Yemeni farmers also grew vegetables and legumes such as radishes, onions, beans, lentils, and leeks. Fruits included mangoes, bananas, apricots, and grapes from the Central Highlands, while dates for export were grown in the Wadi Hadramawt. Northern Yemen was renowned for its honey and mocha coffee. Nonfood crops, in addition to qat, included tobacco and cotton.

Most rural families breed livestock for milk and meat. Women herd cows, and children tend sheep and goats, which provide wool and hides. In the period before 2011, farmers reared chickens in commercial farms, as the demand for eggs had grown.

MOCHA COFFEE

Two hundred years ago, Yemen supplied all of Europe with coffee. It was shipped from the port of Mocha, hence the name "mocha coffee." Even after competitors entered the market, coffee remained Yemen's primary source of foreign exchange. Since the 1970s, however, coffee production has declined because more farmers are growing qat.

In Yemen, as in many other countries around the world, drinking coffee provides a focus at social gatherings. As in other Arab countries, the making and serving of coffee in Yemen constitutes a significant part of showing hospitality to one's guests. There are rituals and skills associated with coffee making and preparation that include roasting the coffee beans and mixing the coffee with fragrant spices.

WOMEN IN AGRICULTURE

When men left for better-paying jobs abroad or in the cities, many rural women carried an extra burden. Women from poorer households are often up at the crack of dawn, cooking for the family and feeding the animals. They might have to collect firewood or fetch water, which often involves a climb into the mountains. Then they tackle the farmwork—sowing seeds, weeding fields, spraying pesticides, plowing, and harvesting. In some families, even old women perform light tasks. The World Economic Forum's 2008 Gender Gap Report ranked Yemen as having the greatest inequality between women and men out of 130 countries.

RESOURCES

The rich fishing waters around Yemen are the country's least developed natural resource. The Red and Arabian Seas are full of mackerel, squid, shrimp, lobster, cuttlefish, and tuna. Most fishermen are small-scale entrepreneurs who lack the money to buy more efficient equipment. Even if more fish were caught, there would not be sufficient processing plants to turn the fish into a valuable

Coffee is native to northern Yemen, Kenya, and Ethiopia. All three countries have similar flora and fauna because they were part of the same landmass until a rift created the Red Sea.

export. There is further concern, in that the Arabian Sea and Indian Ocean suffer periodic fish die-offs, apparently related to lack of oxygen, making fish a potentially unreliable resource.

The discovery of oil reserves in the 1980s brightened Yemen's economic prospects. Commercial extraction began in 1986. Oil wells were opened, and pipelines were built to transport the oil from the fields to the coast. Recently, though, oil production has been gradually declining. Between 2001 and 2007, oil production decreased from 438,500 to 320,600 barrels per day (bpd). While the Yemeni government made plans to increase production from 2009, oil production has instead fallen consistently over the past decade, It was at an all-time low of 11 bpd from January to September of 2017, inching up to a scant 16 bpd in October of 2017. The charts are as dramatic in their decline as charts on climate change are dramatic in their increase.

Yemen mined substantial quantities of salt and marble. Because the country's unique architectural styles require cement, stone, alabaster, and marble, local demand for these commodities is very high. In the midst of the ongoing war, however, data on mining and quarrying are not easily available. Such data ends in 2013 after showing years of slow decline.

Local fishermen fish for shrimp, mackerel, and squid in the Arabian Sea. They do not have the resources needed to buy expensive equipment in order to turn a greater profit.

TOURISM

In times of peace, Yemen has a lot to offer the tourist: a good climate, stunning landscapes with untouched beaches, scuba-diving sites, a cultural heritage with fabulous architecture, and no shortage of historical sites to explore. Yemeni hospitality is unmatched, and the country's customs are fascinating. With sufficient funds and appropriate government guidance, tourist revenue could be a more significant source of income.

To encourage foreign and local investment, the Saleh government modernized business and tourist facilities such as hotels, convention centers, and restaurants. Many, however, were still below international standards at the time of the Arab Spring. It would currently be difficult to make a fair assessment of remaining facilities. Tourism was already hampered by weak infrastructure, unreliable transportation networks, and security concerns. The current state of ongoing civil war makes tourism on the mainland a practical impossibility for the most part.

MANUFACTURING

In 2008, the industrial sector in Yemen accounted for 47 percent of the national output. Oil refining was the most important industry, generating 40 percent of total revenue. The construction industry was growing, along with the manufacture of bricks, tiles, and other building materials. Production included consumer goods, food products such as flour and cooking oil, bottled soft drinks, aluminum houseware products, rubber, and plastics.

The service sector, mainly government and trade services, accounted for 40 percent of Yemen's national output. Public service, distribution, packing, shipping, insurance services, and tourism were expanding.

As in most other developing countries, several deficiencies constrained industrial development: supplies of water and energy were unreliable, the local workforce lacked industrial expertise, and the transportation network was inefficient, with no guarantee that goods were delivered to factories and markets on time.

Like many other economically developing countries, Yemen has relied heavily on its human resources for economic wealth. Yemeni workers were the country's main export for much of the twentieth century. These workers found employment primarily in Saudi Arabia and other Arab states. It is estimated that the remittances sent back to the country by hardworking Yemenis abroad amounted to $3 billion in 2015. Their families used this money to buy goods and services, helping to boost Yemen's economy. In 1990, Saudi Arabia withdrew the right for Yemenis to work in the country and cut off its aid to Yemen, in protest against Yemen's ambiguous stand on Saddam Hussein's invasion of Kuwait, an action that caused the Gulf War. This forced 850,000 Yemenis to return home, which resulted in a massive loss of revenue, record unemployment levels, and economic chaos.

The current situation can't be easily assessed. Unemployment is high—estimated to be as high as 27 percent in 2014, with up to 23 percent of the labor pool made up by child labor. Food insecurity is extreme, with up to 60 percent of the population unsure where their next meals will come from, or when.

ENERGY

Businesses and households need electric power. Energy is needed to run industrial machinery and household appliances. But, for some time, there was not enough energy to go around in Yemen. Energy was expensive, and supplies were unreliable. Locally produced petroleum met some energy requirements, but the country relied on imported fuel and energy. Until the 1960s, Sanaa had no electricity, but by 2009 it had nearly reached the point where everyone in Sanaa had power. Supplying electricity to remote rural areas was costly, so these areas often had to rely on local generators.

To develop the economy, Yemen needed foreign aid. This money, in the form of loans or grants, came from international donors such as the International

Monetary Fund, the World Bank, the European Union, and the United Nations. Economic aid between 2003 and 2007 stood at $2.3 billion. Yemen also tried to encourage foreign investment by offering attractive incentives to potential investors.

Since the Arab Spring uprisings, the nation has suffered ongoing conflict, and its infrastructure has endured much damage. Only approximately 48 percent of the population has had access to electricity during this period of civil war.

INTERNET LINKS

https://www.focus-economics.com/countries/yemen
This site offers an overview of Yemen's economic condition.

http://www.worldbank.org/en/country/yemen
The World Bank offers a serious and objective economic review of Yemen.

ENVIRONMENT

An incense tree emerges from the dry landscape of Socotra. The effects of a serious drought have caused grave environmental and humanitarian concerns.

5

"Mankind's feeling of responsibility to create a decent life and make it worth living with dignity has always been stronger than the will to kill life."
—Tawakkol Karman

PRIOR TO THE CURRENT CIVIL WAR, Yemen had advanced economically at the expense of its ecology. Oil drilling and refining were contaminating the extremely limited natural groundwater, as were untreated sewage and salt. Migratory laborers practiced unsustainable agricultural and hunting practices, depleting the environment before moving on. Most of the natural plants and animals of the region had already been destroyed.

The nation has since had to cope with a growing lack of water resources. Groundwater is limited and is rapidly being used up and not replaced. The reduction in rainfall resulting from climate change increases the problem, as the deep wells of the water table fail to be replenished. Urban areas are running out of water, resulting in desperate attempts to find more resources through deep drilling—a practice that only speeds the day when the water will be entirely gone. Lack of water increases disease and health problems—as does the ongoing civil war.

EROSION AND DESERT

Although agriculture plays an important role in Yemen's economy, its natural environment does not always help support it. Yemen regularly experiences fierce sandstorms and dust storms that cause soil erosion and heavy damage to precious agricultural crops.

Yemen was once covered by lush forests and woodland, but its forested areas have gradually been depleted by overgrazing. The destruction of forests and trees for use as fuel and in the construction industry has also contributed to the problem. The implications of desertification directly affect agricultural workers and bring problems to the general Yemeni population. The most serious consequences of desertification include growing hunger among the population, poor health, and continued poverty. The problem is so serious that, in 2004, Yemen established a national plan to fight against further desertification. This plan has received the support of the Yemeni government and its international partners, including the United Nations desertification program. Unfortunately, for various reasons, including lack of financial support, poor organization, and low rainfall over many years, not all the aims set out in the national plan to prevent desertification were accomplished. The people of Yemen continue to struggle against the effects of desertification today. Yemeni farmers try to combat the problem of desertification by constructing hillside terraces, which can help to reduce soil erosion and conserve water.

WATER

Yemen is a semiarid country with no permanent river systems, only wadis. The country has a comparatively low rainfall of 20 to 31.5 inches (500 to 800 millimeters) a year. The volume of rainfall has been falling on average since 1963. In ancient times, Yemen was the envy of the rest of the Arabian Peninsula for being a lush green land. Since the mid-1990s, however, Yemen's water resources have been slowly depleting. This has been caused mainly by overuse by the agricultural sector and climate change. Today, Yemen is suffering from a dangerous scarcity of water.

The National Water Resources Authority (NWRA) of Yemen estimates that the total renewable freshwater resources for the country are just 88,287 million cubic feet (2,500 million cubic meters) a year. The demand for water in 2009, however, was reported to be 113,007 million cubic feet (3,200 cubic m) a year, which indicates a deficit of 24,720 million cubic feet (700 million cubic m).

The ongoing war and the destruction of infrastructure has made the situation even worse.

Due to the high demand and profitability associated with the growing of qat, an increasing number of agricultural workers are demanding the use of more and more water for irrigating their crops. This increase in demand puts pressure on an already diminished supply of water. As a result of the poor management of water resources, the water crisis continues in the agricultural sector.

Even before the war, urban dwellers who needed water for drinking and other domestic uses were competing with their rural neighbors for the precious supply. In Sanaa, a mere 15 to 25 percent of residents were able to obtain drinking water from the city's official water system. The rest were forced to look elsewhere. The majority purchased their water from private vendors who could be found in the city's streets selling water that they sourced from private wells, as well as from the villages surrounding the city. There were plans to build a series of dams to solve the water shortage. Many feared, however, that this solution was too expensive.

The conflict in Yemen has only intensified the ongoing water crisis. Urban centers like Sanaa are increasingly suffering water shortages, and refugee populations are without water to a degree that endangers the population inside the camps and out.

Refugee populations in Yemen are harmed by the water shortages in the country.

CLIMATE CHANGE

Like many other countries around the world, Yemen has been seriously affected by climate change, including changes in rainfall patterns. In the past, the rainy season used to begin at the start of March. Now, however, it is common for Yemen not to receive rainfall until as late as the end of April. This lack of rainfall is a huge problem for Yemen, causing great hardships especially for its agricultural workers and industries where much water is needed.

In 2008, Yemen's Climate Change Unit at the General Authority of Environment Preservation warned that the continued effects of climate change could even lead to a "catastrophic drought."

Another example of climate change in Yemen can be seen in the increase in average temperatures in Sanaa. There are fears that climate change will cause coastal flooding and that some of the main cities, including the important port of Hodeida, will eventually be submerged by rising seas. Increased temperatures and decreased preciptation, along with the continued conflict in Yemen, have contributed to current food shortages and widespread famine.

DESTRUCTION OF ENVIRONMENT

Air pollution in Yemen is caused by a variety of factors, including the widespread use of heavy construction tools such as industrial saws. The main source of air pollution, however, particularly in cities such as Sanaa, is emissions from cars and other vehicles. In Sanaa alone, there are about 250,000 vehicles, many of

A man walks near a dried-out sewage swamp in the capital city of Sanaa in 2017.

which are very old, having been brought into the country by returning Yemenis after the Gulf War in 1990. The majority of these vehicles use leaded gasoline or local diesel, which contains a high level of impurities. In fact, Yemen remains one of the few countries worldwide that continues to use leaded gasoline in its cars and other vehicles.

Another source of pollution in Yemen, particularly around its coastal areas, is the oil industry. Although oil has historically accounted for a large part of Yemen's revenue, its production, exploration, and transportation have contributed significantly to coastal and maritime pollution in the Red Sea and the Gulf of Aden.

The oil industry isn't responsible for all the pollution of Yemen's marine environment, however. Desalination plants, water-treatment facilities, coastal mining, and quarrying are also responsible for the worsening pollution problems within the marine environment and along the coasts of Yemen.

Yet another cause of marine pollution comes from the increasing use of chemicals in certain agricultural activities. The fertilizers, pesticides, and insecticides used extensively in modern farming end up flowing into the sea and coastal areas, causing damage to the marine life and the surrounding environment.

INTERNET LINKS

https://www.climatelinks.org/resources/climate-change-risk -profile-yemen
This 2016 report includes a summation of the effects and risks of climate change in Yemen.

https://www.unicef.org/yemen/media_12389.html
This UNICEF report offers a view into Yemen's water crisis.

YEMENIS

Young Yemenis have suffered from the many years of conflict and poverty in their country.

Y EMEN IS AN ARAB NATION BEFORE anything else, with a population almost entirely made up of northern and southern tribes. Both are Arab, though they differ in cultural norms. While a wider range of people lived in Yemen prior to the civil conflict, emigration, war, illness, and genocide have dramatically changed the demographics of the country. In particular, some Islamic groups have attacked Christian and Jewish communities, leaving serious questions as to whether any members of these groups remain alive in the country at this time.

6

The creativity and skilled craftsmanship of the Yemeni Jews had a major impact on the indigenous non-Jewish culture. When the Jews departed, many traditional crafts disappeared.

POPULATION STATISTICS

With a population of approximately 28 million, Yemen is one of the most densely populated areas in the Arabian Peninsula. In comparison, neighboring Oman has a population of only 4.6 million. Saudi Arabia has a population of 28.5 million, but its land area is four times the size of Yemen. The average population density in Yemen is 135.33 people per square mile (52.25 people per square kilometer) as of 2016. The majority of Yemenis

The Western perception of the traditional Arab is of the Bedouin. The Bedouin are nomadic camel-breeding tribes of herders who roam the deserts. But the majority of the tribes in Yemen are not nomadic but are farmers and city dwellers. Only an estimated 1 percent of the population are Bedouin, and they are concentrated in the eastern governorates, especially al-Mahrah.

The Bedouin have always been fiercely proud of their freedom and ability to survive with the bare necessities: their livestock, a tent, a rug, and a few cooking pots. Despite their remarkable independence, they have never lived in total isolation. Throughout history, they have sold their thoroughbred camels to villagers and townspeople and have purchased items that they could not produce themselves, including a few luxuries such as tobacco.

Today, many Bedouin have settled or gone to work in the oil fields. Others still lead a more traditional lifestyle, but the tracks of four-wheel-drive vehicles that cut through the desert are telltale signs of change.

live in small villages scattered across the countryside. About 36 percent live in cities or towns, and this percentage is increasing as the country develops. Around 40 percent of the population is below the age of fifteen.

ARABS

The majority of Yemenis are Arabs, but they divide themselves into two groups based on their genealogy. The first group, the southern Arabs, are sons of Qahtan, and they originated in Yemen. Qahtan is recorded as having been the son of Shem and the grandson of Noah. The Hashid and Bakil tribal groups trace their ancestry from Qahtan and are said to be related to the ancient

Sabeans. The second group, the northern Arabs, are the "sons of Adnan." Adnan is the Islamic version of the biblical Ishmael, one of Abraham's sons. Sayyids, who are members of Yemen's religious elite, are northern Arabs. Historians confirm that both groups have been in Arabia from the earliest known times.

Throughout most of their history, the Arabs of the interior have not been exposed to intruders because the desert and the sea kept out foreign influences. There is more racial mixing in the towns and the seaports. For example, some of the people living along the Red Sea are of African descent.

THE LOSS OF YEMENI JEWS

For centuries, Jews were the largest non-Muslim group living permanently in Yemen. Most of them were descendants of indigenous people who adopted Judaism in pre-Islamic times. When the state of Israel was founded in 1948, many Jews left Yemen. Almost half of the population in Sanaa used to be

Jewish Yemeni musicians perform during the holdiday of Sukkot in 2005.

Jewish. Before the war, there were just a few thousand Jews left in the whole country, mainly elderly and living in mountain villages. Houthi rebels targeted the last remaining Yemeni Jews in a program of ethnic cleansing, and it is not known if any remain today in the country.

SOCIAL HIERARCHY

The massive disruption caused by the ongoing conflict has altered exactly how the Yemeni people live in ways that are unlikely to become clear for years to come. It remains to be seen how much traditional Yemeni social structure continues in the midst of war, how much will recover after war, and how much has been destroyed or altered beyond recognition.

Yemenis are divided into groups depending on their tribal lineage.

Yemenis have traditionally been stratified by ancestry, distinguishing those of high religious status from the tribal farmers and those who worked in the marketplace. At the apex of the social pyramid are the sayyids, who are descendants of the prophet Muhammad. The lineage of the Prophet has great importance in Islam, particularly in India, Pakistan, and Yemen. During the Zaidi imamate, the sayyids held important government positions and were wealthy landlords. Because of their education, religious knowledge, and administrative expertise, sayyids are respected to this day. Quite a number of them are teachers, healers, and mediators in tribal disputes.

Another elite group are the qadis: Islamic scholars of law. Their status is also hereditary, and they have historically served as a minor gentry class. Many members of elite qadi families have played important roles in Yemen's history. An example would be Abdul Rahman al-Iryani, president of the former Yemen Arab Republic.

Tribal people of Qahtani ancestry fall below the elite groups in terms of social status. The Qahtani are mostly farmers. Each tribal unit is headed by a sheikh, who is traditionally supposed to be a wise man of good character.

The sheikh oversees village affairs and may sometimes act as a government official. The members of a tribe have a strong sense of belonging, and each tribe has its own characteristic dress, poetry, dance, and cuisine.

Below the tribal people are those members of society of unrecognized descent. These people perform various services—they may be butchers, barbers, or wedding musicians. At the bottom of the social pyramid are those who perform menial jobs such as sweeping the streets. In the past, these people were social outcasts.

People's attitudes have been changing in recent years. As a result, the traditional social hierarchy is blurring.

"Look to your neighbor rather than your distant brother." —Yemeni proverb

RURAL AND URBAN LIFE

In Yemen, the division between rural and urban populations is an important social distinction. The tribal people are rural folk who work in the agricultural sector; the sayyids, the qadis, and those employed in trade, commerce, or manufacturing industries perceive themselves as city folk.

There is a bit of good-natured competition between the urban and the rural people. The tribal people consider city folk to be weaker and less healthy, and some city folk consider the rural people to be less sophisticated.

MEN'S WEAR

The saying "you are what you wear" is descriptive of traditional male attire in Yemen. Clothing identifies where a man comes from, his tribe, and his position in society. The type of headgear and the way it is worn, and the appearance and position of a man's dagger, are important too.

Traditional male tribal dress consists of a *futa* (FOO-ta), which is a wraparound skirt; a handwoven turban; and a *jambiya* (JAHM-bi-yah), which is a ceremonial dagger. The dagger is worn upright and centered and is kept in place by a leather or cloth belt. You can tell the status of a man by the design and the materials used to make his dagger. You can tell which tribe a man belongs to by the way he wraps his turban around his head.

Three Yemeni men display their tribal dress.

In addition, a man might wear a short coat made of woven wool or sheepskin. A shawl thrown over the shoulders keeps him warm and can also be used as a handy tote bag.

Today, dress patterns are changing. In the cities, more men are wearing suits, ties, and other forms of Western-style clothing. Traditional clothing is often combined with Western-style shirts and blazers, and colorful imported cloth covers the head. Many Yemeni men, both in the cities and in rural areas, wear more traditional Arab clothing that consists of cotton breeches or a striped kilt. Many men wear skullcaps, turbans, or tall, round hats called tarbooshes.

WOMEN'S WEAR

In Yemen, women dress to reflect their regional and social status. The regional variation in clothing styles among Yemeni women is fantastic; rural and urban women also dress quite differently.

Many Yemeni women wear loose, long tunics or dresses; the majority cover their heads with shawls and veils. Most women wear leg coverings such as bloomers, slacks, or dark tights under their dresses or tunics. Their clothing is a regional variation of the nearly universal *salwar kameez* (tunic and trousers) and robes common to much of Islam.

In many urban and even in some rural areas, women have adopted Western dress. At home, younger women wear jeans, T-shirts, and

A Yemeni woman wears a *dhola* while aiding a calf as it drinks its mother's milk.

sweaters. For special occasions, such as religious festivals or weddings, women wear their loveliest outfits and traditional jewelry. Glittering silver adorns the neck, the ankles, the wrists, and sometimes the forehead.

Women dress modestly, according to Muslim dictates, and often veil themselves in the presence of strange men. The veiling of women is not a law in Yemen as it is in Saudi Arabia. Some younger, educated women in urban areas cover their heads but not their faces. There are a few women who choose not to wear a veil at all. For a brief period in socialist South Yemen, urban women chose to adopt a Western style of dress and rejected the veil. Since unification, however, the majority of women in Yemen have worn a head covering in response to growing conservatism.

Outer head coverings among urban and rural women are different. Rural women may wear one or more scarves on their head and a woolen shawl for weddings or when traveling beyond their village. Rural women frequently wear a broad-brimmed straw hat called a *dhola* (DOH-ler) to protect themselves from the sun while working outdoors.

Most urban women in Yemen wear a face veil or an *abaya*.

In the Tihama, many women are not veiled. They wear hats woven from palm fronds, resembling those worn in Mexico. Women in the mountains drape sprigs of sweet-smelling basil over their ears for decoration or to protect against the evil eye or evil spirits.

Most urban women wear a face veil and are frequently enveloped in a *sharshaf* (SHAHR-shahf), which is a loose, black garment that covers the body, or are gracefully attired in a *sitara* (SEE-tahr-a), a brightly colored covering. Another common covering is the *abaya*, worn by women in many other Arab countries: a loose black robe that covers the women from head to toe. Professional urban women wear a headscarf and a coat. The hijab, a headscarf that covers the hair and the neck, is also popular.

BODY PAINTING

Despite the influx of European cosmetics, women and girls still paint themselves with traditional makeup for special occasions. Before a religious festival, women will paint black floral designs on their hands and feet with a substance called khidab *(KEY-dab).*

In Sanaa, it is customary for a bride to be embellished by an experienced body painter before her wedding. The ink is applied to the body with a needle, an acacia thorn, or even a toothpick. The face and the neck are decorated, as are the arms from the hands to the shoulders and the legs from the feet to the knees. Although there are catalogs containing various patterns, an experienced body painter uses her imagination to create vivid designs. This ritual takes several hours and a lot of patience!

INTERNET LINKS

https://www.apogeephoto.com/yemeni-dress-photographing-the -culture-and-customs
This website features beautiful photographs of Yemeni regional dress as current as 2016.

https://www.timesofisrael.com/yemeni-minister-says-fate-of -countrys-remaining-jews-unknown
This article examines the fate of Yemeni Jews in the civil war.

http://www.worldometers.info/world-population/yemen -population
This site offers population information for countries around the world, including Yemen.

LIFESTYLE

Yemeni children have born the brunt of years of civil conflict and resource scarcity.

YEMEN IS A LAND WITH DEEP ROOTS and ancient traditions. These traditional ways have been under pressure in recent years, due both to globalization and civil conflict. Today, the best word to describe the current lifestyle throughout much of the country is "chaotic." War, ethnic cleansing, and food scarcity have created an unstable situation in which most Yemenis are struggling just to survive. Despite the difficulties that the country and its people face, however, Yemeni culture remains a powerful force among its people—a force upon which Yemenis depend in the midst of continued instability and chaos.

CULTURAL VALUES

Most responsibilities are shared among relatives, friends, and neighbors. When someone goes on a trip, a neighbor might take care of essential tasks such as tending the livestock. If anyone is missing from a gathering,

7

"Before, I had everything to eat, everything. I was happy, at ease. Now you can't even have one cake."
—Ahmed Abdu, nine-year-old Yemeni boy

Life in rural Yemen typically involves greater social interaction, as daily tasks are often preformed with others.

a friend or a neighbor will drop by to ensure that everything is all right. When two people are arguing in the street, a bystander may step in to mediate.

Yemenis are well known for their politeness, hospitality, and generosity, especially toward guests and those less fortunate. Perhaps the Queen of Sheba started the tradition of hospitality when she showered King Solomon with gifts.

A guest is honored and welcomed as though part of the family. The host labors to ensure that visitors feel at home, plying them with plenty of food, drink, gifts, and entertainment. This generosity is not confined to the home. For example, when a Yemeni is eating in front of another, he or she will always offer to share the food.

TIME FOR PLEASANTRIES

Human relationships are extremely important in Yemen. Whether in a mountain village or in the city, people always have time to exchange a smile and a greeting.

People in the villages live in close proximity, especially in the mountains, where the houses are huddled together. There is plenty of social interaction, as daily chores are rarely performed in isolation; there is always time to chat with one's neighbors.

In the cities, life is faster, more cosmopolitan, and less personal. Yet people still approach their work differently than most urban Westerners do. When conducting business, a period of time is always devoted to exchanging family news.

The common phrase *insha Allah* (EEN-sha Allah), which means "God willing," reveals the Yemeni attitude that time and deadlines are flexible—a matter of God's rule, not human planning.

In both the cities and the countryside, men and women get together (in separate groups) in the afternoons to sip tea, chew qat, and chat. During the years before the war, a number of city offices closed for these afternoon gatherings.

THE YEMENI FAMILY

Before the war, an average Yemeni family consisted of a whole collection of relatives who lived under the same roof. Very few people in Yemen lived on their own. Grandparents, widows, and divorcees were all taken under the family wing. However, the number of family members living under the same roof has decreased in recent years.

In Yemeni culture, there is a prescribed order regulating family life. Each family member has a specific role and responsibility based on his or her age and sex. For both men and women, authority is based on seniority. The elderly command the utmost respect, and their opinions are highly valued. They are often asked to mediate in disputes.

In more patriarchal families, the men generally assume tasks that require contact with the public, such as shopping in the market for household provisions. Women cook, clean, and do the washing. Younger and fitter women also do the more strenuous work, such as carrying water and fetching fuel. In urban areas, the traditional roles within a family were changing before the war as more women went to work.

A large family is valued in rural areas of Yemen, where children are expected to aid in daily chores.

CHILDREN

To Yemenis, children are gifts from God and are welcomed after marriage. Many women deliver babies at home, assisted by an older female family members or a midwife.

A large family is highly valued in rural areas because there are more people to help with the many chores. Children have to help look after their younger siblings and harvest the crops. Increasing poverty and difficulty making a living from the land, though, caused more women to choose to have smaller families so that they could afford to educate their children for nonagricultural jobs.

Yemeni parents are proud of their children and raise them in a loving environment. Girls are taught to be patient, loving, modest, and helpful. Boys learn that they must protect the women of their family and uphold the family honor. The children are taught skills required for an urban or a rural life from their parents, grandparents, and older brothers and sisters.

ARRANGED MARRIAGES

Most marriages are arranged by the families of the prospective couple, but they are rarely forced. Family members play an important part in matchmaking and bringing suitable couples together. In a small town, a young man might know a girl by sight, but he would have few chances of meeting her, as there is a greater segregation of the sexes than in Western countries. Therefore he would have to rely on the advice of his mother or sister, who would know the women of the neighborhood well. The mother plays a significant part in choosing a suitable wife for her son.

A Yemeni wedding

In more traditional communities, once she has decided on a girl, normally based on her dignity and status, a mother would confer with her husband. If both parents agree on the choice, they consult with their son. After a prospective wife has been chosen, father and son would pay a visit to the house of the bride's family to speak to her father. However, the decision is not made right away. The potential father-in-law has to think it over and discuss the matter with his daughter. Only when everybody agrees is a date fixed for the betrothal.

Betrothal is an informal affair. Father and son, along with a few male relatives, deliver a number of gifts, such as raisins, dates, clothes, and qat, to the bride's house. They also give the engagement ring to the girl's father for safekeeping. Then they discuss suitable dates for the wedding and agree on a bride price, which is usually paid in cash.

TOWER HOUSES

A tower house is a multistory house with many attractively decorated rooms. Each family unit has its own room or story, while certain communal areas are

According to some interpretations of the Quran, a Muslim man is permitted to marry up to four women, provided he can care for them equally. Not all Muslims accept this, and most Yemeni men have only one wife.

shared. The ground floor is usually used for storage. Families live on the upper stories, where there are bedrooms, sitting rooms, dining areas, kitchens, and bathrooms. People often sleep in different rooms depending on the season, occupying the warmest ones in winter. The elderly are given light and airy rooms to make them more comfortable. The rooms are usually furnished similarly, with a chest or a trunk for a person's personal items and some wooden pegs for hanging clothes.

Tower houses are typical across urban areas of Yemen.

The best room in the house, the *mafraj* (MAHF-rahj), is also the highest. It is therefore perfect for enjoying a view of Yemen's dreamy landscapes. The walls are often whitewashed and decorated with delicate patterns and verses of poetry. The floor may be covered with mattresses, carpets, and decorative cushions. This is where socializing, entertaining, and other leisure activities take place. Afternoons are spent here eating snacks, chewing qat, listening to music, and exchanging the latest news.

Male strangers are supposed to stay out of the areas used by women. If they have to pass the women's quarters on the way to the mafraj, they call out "Allah Allah" to announce their approach, so that the women can shut their doors or cover their faces.

Building techniques for these distinctive tower houses have been passed down from generation to generation. Many Arabic houses are built around a secluded courtyard. Yemeni houses, however, are usually built to face outward, often overlooking a public space or street. The exterior walls of many of these tower houses have been exquisitely decorated with ancient motifs including Sabean script, intricate geometric patterns, and ancient symbols of snakes and water.

EDUCATION

Until the 1960s, formal education was primarily the privilege of the elite members of Yemeni society. Many children were schooled in the village mosque,

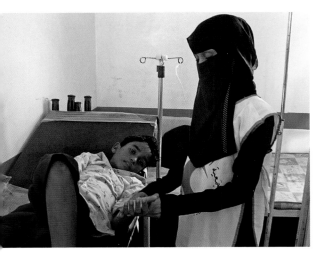

A Yemeni health care worker examines her patient.

where instruction was oral and the emphasis was on memorizing the Quran rather than learning to read and write. A lucky few went to Aden or Egypt to be educated, but many children remained illiterate.

During the period of unification, everyone was felt to have the right to an elementary education, which was free and compulsory. Children started elementary school at six years of age and finished at fifteen. After this, some children continued their studies in secondary school, until the age of eighteen. Before the war, males received an average of eleven years of education, while females received an average of seven years.

Unfortunately, the civil war has greatly disrupted the education system in Yemen. As of November 2017, between 12,000 and 14,400 schools were closed in Yemen, and many teachers remain unpaid. More school closings were expected to come. Education is currently in the hands of families, communities, and charities. Concerns regarding the spreading of diseases like cholera also stymie education in the country.

HEALTH CARE

As of 2014, Yemen's expenditure on health as a percentage of its GDP stood at 5.6 percent. Yemen's life expectancy, as of 2017, was sixty-four years for males and sixty-eight years for females. The United States, in comparison, spent 17.4 percent of its GDP on health in 2014. Life expectancy in the United States is seventy-six years for males and eighty-one years for females.

Since the civil war, it has become impossible to speak easily about health in Yemen. The country is in crisis, with rampant disease and violence causing chaos on its population. In December 2017, a cholera outbreak infected one million people; thousands have since died from the disease. This is largely due to the fact that Yemen's health-care system has collapsed. Less than 45 percent of hospitals in Yemen are operational, and many health workers risk their lives to help those in need.

Yemen was the first country on the Arabian Peninsula to grant women the right to vote.

ANCIENT MEDICINE

There is an ancient body of medical literature in Yemen. Some of this knowledge is based on the findings of the ancient Egyptians and Greeks. The Greeks believed that the human body consisted of four elements: earth, fire, air, and water. The combination of these elements in a person's body was supposed to give them a particular "temperament," and one had to balance these elements in order to stay healthy.

A distinctive Islamic medical tradition grew out of these principles and built on the practices of the prophet Muhammad and his companions regarding health and sickness. These practices stressed the importance of fresh air, exercise, and diet. Hot, fatty foods were to be eaten in October, for example, while cold, wet foods such as fish and sour milk were recommended for June.

INTERNET LINKS

https://www.chathamhouse.org/expert/comment/yemen-s-health-crisis-how-world-s-largest-cholera-outbreak-unfolded
This Chatham House article examines how the cholera outbreak began in Yemen.

https://www.uae-medical-insurance.com/resources/yemen-topics/overview
This site explains Yemen's health-care system.

http://www.who.int/bulletin/volumes/93/10/15-021015/en
This World Health Organization bulletin examines the health crisis in Yemen.

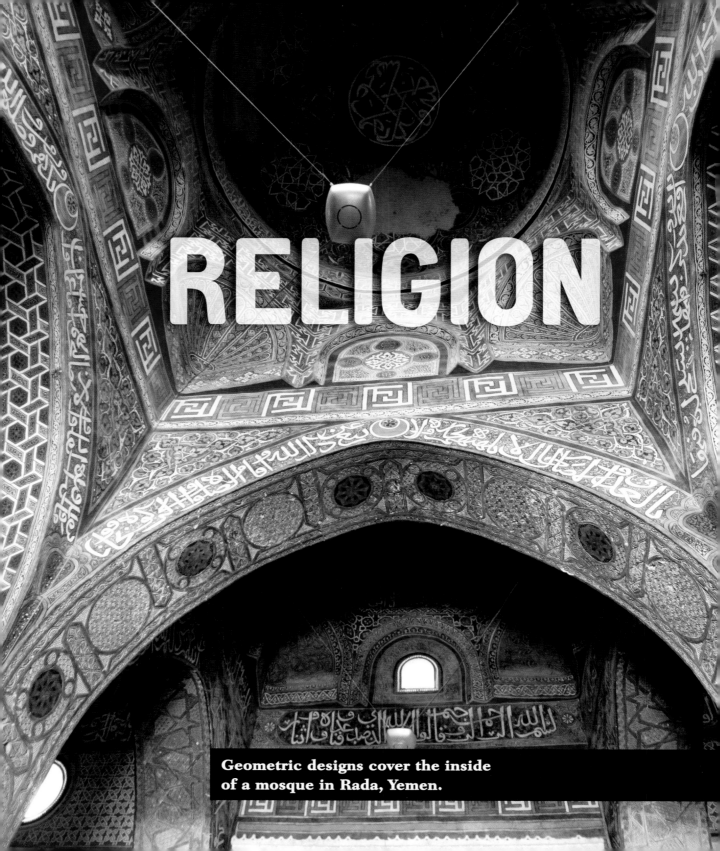

RELIGION

Geometric designs cover the inside of a mosque in Rada, Yemen.

8

ISLAM IS THE THIRD OF THE GREAT world religions to flower out of the Middle East. The first, Judaism, gave rise to Christianity, and both together brought forth Islam.

Yemen is demographically Islamic, with very few other religions represented in the country. While the nation is limited in the diversity of its religions outside Islam, it is currently divided by conflicting factions and sects of Islam. The primary division is the Sunni-Shia schism present throughout Islam. Wahabist factions such as al-Qaeda are also present in the country.

THE PROPHET MUHAMMAD

Muhammad was born in Mecca, an important trading and cultural center in Saudi Arabia, in 570 CE. Even as a boy, Muhammad disliked the largely animistic tribal beliefs of his fellow Arabs. When he was older, he became a traveling merchant. He was successful, but disturbed by the greed around him, he often retreated to the mountains to think. At the age of twenty-five, he married a noblewoman, Khadija, and they had six children.

When Muhammad was forty, a profound experience changed his life. According to Islamic tradition, the angel Gabriel appeared to Muhammad one night, and for more than twenty years thereafter communicated God's words to him. These revelations concerned issues of religion, government, human conduct, and relationships.

Encouraged by his wife, Muhammad began preaching to the people of Mecca, urging them to abandon the idols they worshipped and lead better lives. The city's establishment first became concerned, then hostile,

"Abu Abdullah (al-Bukhari) said, 'Yemen was called so because it is situated to the right of the Ka'ba, and Sham was called so because it is situated to the left of the Ka'ba.'" —Saheeh Al-Bukhari, from *The Virtues and Merits of the Prophet and his Companions*

When using English, the Islamic tradition is to put the initials "pbuh" in parenthesis after naming the prophet Mohammed. The initials stand for "peace be upon him," or "sallallahu alayhi wa sallam," in the original Arabic. Similar initials are used when using other alphabets and other languages. The phrase is intended to mark both respect and affection for the Prophet. Many use the same honorifics when writing of Jesus, as Islam considers Jesus one of God's prophets.

as Muhammad's following grew. Muhammad and his followers fled north to Medina in 622 CE. This became known as the Hegira, or the year of migration, and it is year one of the Islamic calendar.

In Medina, the Muslim community continued to grow stronger. By 630 CE, Muslims had returned to Mecca and conquered the city that had exiled them years before. Islam continued to spread throughout the Middle East and beyond.

Today, Muslims are found all over the world. They may be Arabs, Indonesians, Indians, Africans, Americans, or other nationalities. Islam has historically accepted converts of all ethnicities and nations.

SUNNI AND SHIA

When Muhammad died in 632 CE, one of his close friends, Abu Bakr, was chosen to lead the Muslim community. This led to some discontent in the community among those who believed Muhammad's son-in-law, Ali, should have been appointed to lead. Sometime after Abu Bakr's death, a group called the Shia refused to accept one of the later successors. As a result, a major split developed within Islam. The division between Shiism and Sunnism remains to this day. Both divisions agree on most of the major matters of faith and worship, but some of their laws are different.

HOLY TEXTS

The Islamic faith is based on the Quran, a book of God's words spoken through the prophet Muhammad. Muslims accept the Bible but believe that the Quran is the supreme source of divine instruction.

The Quran is divided into 114 suras, or chapters, which have multiple verses. Muslims try to memorize as many verses as they can. Special status and honor is given to those who memorize the Quran completely. Those who have done so are known as *hafiz*, or guardians, because they add to the safeguards protecting the scripture.

Muslims believe that the life of Muhammad embodied the teachings of the Quran, and his life is therefore another source of guidance. Many of his

sayings were memorized and preserved by his companions. The Hadith is a collection of these sayings. The Sunna refers to the way of life prescribed for Muslims on the basis of the teachings and practices of Muhammad and interpretations of the Quran.

A young student studies the Quran at his mosque.

THE FIVE PILLARS

Besides accepting Islam's beliefs, a Muslim must fulfill a list of religious duties. These duties play an important part in maintaining a sense of belonging to the Muslim community. They are commonly known as the Five Pillars of Islam.

1. *Shahadah* (sha-HAHD-a) is profession and the essence of a Muslim's faith. It involves reciting two statements: "There is no God but God" and "Muhammad is the prophet of God." Muslims repeat these statements daily in prayer. The belief

"What you sow, so shall ye reap."
—Yemeni proverb

According to
Islamic tradition,
all Muslims
should give alms
before the end
of Ramadan.
Almsgiving is
supposed to purify
the giver's soul.

that Muhammad is God's ultimate messenger is a key element distinguishing Islam from Judaism and Christianity.

2. *Salat* (sa-LAHT) is prayer. A Muslim must pray five times a day, at sunrise, midday, midafternoon, sunset, and night. Prayers can be performed anywhere—at school, at work, at home, outdoors—but there is a prescribed form. Before praying, Muslims must be in a state of mental and physical purity. They cleanse their mouths. Then they wash their face, neck, hands, arms, and feet.

Praying involves reciting parts of the Quran, bowing, kneeling, and touching the head to the ground, symbolizing submission to God. Some Muslims kneel on a prayer rug as they pray. When they pray, Muslims face Mecca, the spiritual center of Islam. Mecca is where the central shrine of pilgrimage for Muslims, the Kaaba, lies. The Kaaba is a small stone building that houses the Black Stone. Muslims believe that this stone fell from paradise when Adam and Eve were cast out.

Muslims circle around the Kaaba in Mecca, Saudi Arabia.

PURIFICATION

Ritual purity is a fundamental requirement of Islam. Prayer has no value unless one has purified oneself in mind and body beforehand. According to the Quran, water is the beginning of life and should be used for purifying the body. Wherever there is water, there is usually a place of prayer. In the highlands of Yemen, worshippers gather around streams and ponds to make their ablutions and pray. In the cities, worshippers frequently purify themselves in bathhouses. Almost every mosque has an ablution pool. However, water is not always easy to come by. In such cases, the worshipper can make the ablution with sand or simply go through the motions with the hands.

3. *Zakat* (za-KAHT) is almsgiving. According to the Quran, one is supposed to give up one's "surplus." So the third pillar involves giving a certain percentage of one's wealth to the poor and needy.

4. *Sawm* (sa-AHM) is fasting. All Muslims are expected to go without food or drink during the daylight hours of the month of Ramadan. Everyone is required to fast except small children, the elderly, nursing mothers, and the infirm. Those traveling may refrain from fasting, but they must make up the days at a later date. Life slows nearly to a standstill during Ramadan, and many shops stay closed until after the midday prayers. Muslims believe that during Ramadan, the gates of paradise are opened and the gates of hell are closed, and the sins of those who fast will be forgiven. This is a time of religious contemplation. Muslims stay up late at night to read the Quran, and they visit the mosque more often than usual. At the end of the month there is a great festival with rich food and presents. This is known as Eid al-Fitr, a celebration of the breaking of the fast.

5. *Hajj* (HAHJ) is pilgrimage to Mecca. At least once in a lifetime, Muslims who can afford it should travel to the holy city of Mecca. The pilgrimage represents an act of obedience to God and should be made in the twelfth and last month of the Islamic year. Eid al-Adha, or the Feast of the Sacrifice, marks the last

The hajj is not just a trip to Mecca. Numerous rituals must be performed. Muslims prepare themselves by studying these under a religious leader. At a certain point on the road to Mecca, pilgrims must purify themselves, don the hajj garments, and proclaim their intention to make the pilgrimage. Upon arrival, they pray at the Great Mosque and walk around the Kaaba seven times, touching or kissing the Black Stone. Afterward, they visit other holy sites in the vicinity.

Other rites include running between the hills of Safa and Marwa; drinking from the well of Zamzam; and standing for most of the day in meditation at Mount Arafat, where Muhammad gave a famous sermon. On the way back to Mecca, Muslims stop at Mina to perform another symbolic act known as stoning the devil. Small stones about the size of peas are thrown at pillars that represent the temptations of Satan.

The pilgrimage concludes with the sacrifice of an animal, usually a sheep, a goat, or a camel. To signify the successful completion of the hajj, the ritual ablution involves snipping a few locks of hair and trimming the nails.

Women as well as men are obligated to perform the hajj, but there are some particular rules imposed upon them. The most limiting is the obligation to be accompanied by a husband or a man of such close relation as to exclude the possibility of marriage. If a woman has no such man to accompany her on hajj, her obligation is eliminated, and she receives no blame for failing to perform her pilgrimage.

day of the pilgrimage, which lasts ten days. Those who cannot fulfill the hajj in the time of Eid al-Adha often take what is called the "lesser pilgrimage," *umrah*—a pilgrimage to Mecca at any other time of the year to perform the rituals of hajj.

MOSQUES

When Muhammad and his followers arrived in Medina in 622 CE, there was no suitable place where they could worship. Therefore they gathered in Muhammad's house to listen to his sermons and to pray. His house became known as a *masjid* (MAHS-jid), which is Arabic for "mosque." This is a place of prayer and worship, as well as a place of rest and study.

Traditional mosques are rectangular and built of brick, stone, or whatever material is locally available. There is a slender minaret, from which the muezzin, or mosque official, gives the call for Muslims to pray.

A minaret emerges from a mosque in Yemen.

Mosques have similar features. There is a courtyard with a place for worshippers to wash and leave their shoes. Inside the prayer hall is a special niche in one wall indicating the direction of Mecca. There is also a pulpit for the prayer leader. The prayer hall is a single large room with carpets for worshippers to kneel on. There are usually other rooms for study groups.

Many mosques are richly decorated with geometric designs and verses from the Quran. In most mosques there are no religious scenes of God or Muhammad, as the majority of Muslim communities forbid the use of representational images.

Male worshippers pray at their mosque. Muslims are expected to pray five times per day.

PRAYER AND DAILY LIFE

Muslims divide their day according to the five obligatory prayer times. At dawn, the muezzin makes the first call to prayer. The first person to wake rouses the rest of the family. Once out of bed, the men, often clad in the same white robes they wear as nightshirts, will set off for the mosque. The women usually pray in the privacy of their home. After morning prayer, the daily routine begins. Children get ready for school, and the women begin the day's cooking. The men, and the women, too, if they have jobs outside the home, get ready for work.

When the sun reaches its peak, the muezzin calls the faithful for the midday prayer. After prayer, family members meet for lunch and then return to their daily activities.

When the sun is at a forty-five-degree angle to the earth, it is time for the afternoon prayer. The sunset prayer signals that it is time for the women to return to their homes. After the sunset prayer, the family eats supper. There is a little time for homework, watching television, or listening to the radio until the evening prayer. Then it is time for bed.

INTERNET LINKS

https://www.irishtimes.com/news/world/middle-east/how-yemen-slid-from-territorial-disputes-to-religious-war-1.2978108
This article from the *Irish Times* looks into the religious aspect of the current civil conflict.

https://www.state.gov/j/drl/rls/irf/2010/148855.htm
This US State Department brief explains how religion influences politics in Yemen.

https://www.worldatlas.com/articles/religious-beliefs-in-yemen.html
This World Atlas site explains popular religious beliefs in Yemen.

LANGUAGE

While Modern Standard Arabic is the standard written form of the language, Yemenis speak various Arabic dialects.

9

"Having a clear tongue is better than having goods you can't manage."
—Yemeni proverb

ARABIC IS THE PRIMARY LANGUAGE of the Arabian Peninsula. It is believed to have developed in Saudi Arabia approximately two thousand years ago among the nomadic Arab tribes of the region.

Arabic is fluid, expressive, and artistic. It is classified as a macrolanguage because it is comprised of many regional variants. The standard written form is known as Modern Standard Arabic, which is rarely spoken and is derived from Classical Arabic—the language of the Quran.

ARABIC

Arabic belongs to the Hamito-Semitic family of languages. More specifically, Arabic belongs to the Semitic group of languages and is closely related to Hebrew, the language of the Jews. Arabic was first spoken two thousand years ago by people living on the Arabian Peninsula.

With the expansion of Islam, the Arabic language spread to other parts of the world. From its birthplace on the Arabian Peninsula, Islam spread east and west. At its zenith, the use of the Arabic language extended from Spain, across North Africa, and onward to Central Asia and India. Today, more than 313 million people speak Arabic. It is the official language of many countries in North Africa and the Middle East.

ALPHABET AND NUMERALS

There is a great deal of discussion as to when the Arabic alphabet was invented. Some believe it was developed in the fourth century CE, while others believe it was earlier. It has twenty-eight characters and is written and read from right to left. There are no capital letters, but the shape of a letter changes depending on its position in a word. Arabic script has a rich variety of forms and makes for magnificent calligraphic decoration. The ancient Kufic script, which is heavy and angular, was used in the earliest copies of the Quran.

A few of the sounds used in Arabic have no equivalent in the English language, and most vowels are not written. Therefore an Arabic word can be rendered in English in a variety of ways. For example, both Muslim and Moslem are perfectly legitimate, as are Muhammad, Mohammed, and Mehemet.

The numbers the western world uses today are derived from Arabic numerals, which are shown on this clock.

The numbers that we use today come from the Arabs. Long ago, the Christian world used Roman numerals, where letters represent numbers. For example, the letter C is 100, and the letter M is 1,000. The numbers 0, 1, 2, 3, 4, 5, 6, 7, 8, and 9, which are so familiar to us, are known as Arabic numerals, though the Arabs learned them originally from India. Traders and merchants brought this Arabic number system across the Mediterranean and into Spain. From Spain, it spread throughout Europe.

SCRIPT

The language used for writing throughout the Arab world is known as Classical Arabic. It is an ancient language, modeled after the language of the Quran. Classical Arabic has changed very little over the centuries.

Poets and writers used Classical Arabic in the early Islamic period. It is considered the most eloquent form of Arabic. All Muslims, regardless of their

native tongue, perform their recitations in Classical Arabic because they believe that to translate the words of God from that sacred language would be impious.

Classical Arabic is a difficult language to read, even for those who speak it. Moreover, it lacks many words necessary in today's world. As a result, a simplified version of Classical Arabic, known as Modern Standard Arabic, was developed in the last century. It is much easier to read and allows for the expression of modern concepts. Children in all Arab countries learn to read and write Modern Standard Arabic.

Arabic calligraphy is an important art form across the Muslim world.

SPEECH

Although Arabs share a common written language, variations in the spoken word have evolved over time. Today, spoken Arabic, also known as colloquial

Many alphabetic scripts used along the Mediterranean coastline are traceable to the Phoenician alphabet of about 1000 BCE. Two variations of the Phoenician script, known as the North and the South Arabian scripts, were in use on the Arabian Peninsula around 500 BCE. The South Arabian script was also called the Sabean script, named after the legendary kingdom of Saba, or Sheba. With the decline of the kingdom of Saba, the script fell into disuse, and the Arabic used today did not come from the Sabeans.

Arabic, consists of five main groups of dialects: Syrian, Arabian, North African, Iraqi, and Egyptian. Some of these are mutually unintelligible. Although two literate Arabs can communicate by using Classical Arabic, most Yemenis would find it difficult to converse with a Moroccan. Local dialects also vary within a country. In Yemen, certain Arabic letters are pronounced differently in the north than they are in the south.

The Arabic language is an emotional one and has a powerful effect on its users. Arabs love the harmony of word combinations and often concern themselves more with the impact of words than with their meaning. Because of the nature of the language, there is a tendency toward exaggeration, repetition, and the use of metaphors and similes, all of which produce an even stronger effect.

BODY LANGUAGE

A Yemeni is almost as physically expressive as he is verbally expressive. When talking, Yemenis stand close together and look each other in the eye. It is quite common for members of the same sex to touch each other while talking. A man might clasp another's hand or touch his shoulder. This is the Yemeni way of showing respect and affection. Even the position of the feet is significant. Yemenis attach great importance to manners, so it is best not to point the soles of your feet at one of them; they consider this act to be extremely insulting.

"From a pound of talk, an ounce of understanding."
—Yemeni proverb

FREE PRESS

Yemen's press and media, once among the freest in the Arab world, have become polarized since the start of the current civil war. The country's formerly strong English-language press has almost disappeared. Television and radio dominate the field, providing easy access to native speakers and broadcast capabilities that reduce distribution problems.

While Yemen's press was once one of the freest in the Arab world, civil conflict has affected the availability and independence of the media.

INTERNET LINKS

https://www.arabacademy.com
This site offers beginning courses in Arabic.

http://arabicwithoutwalls.ucdavis.edu/aww
This site provides basic information about Arabic and teaching Arabic.

https://www.britannica.com/topic/Arabic-language
This Encyclopedia Britannica website offers historical information on Arabic.

ARTS

A Yemeni man works inside his brass-crafting shop in the Old City of Sanaa.

10

YEMEN HAS A POWERFUL ARTISTIC voice that continues even during the civil war. Yemeni art has become a source of courage, laughter, and solidarity for citizens suffering chaos and violence.

Yemen, like many other Arab nations, has historically been intensely artistic. The architecture of Yemen prior to the current conflict was both beautiful and functional. Islamic art and calligraphy graced buildings and books. Yemeni poets have been powerful artists for centuries, providing courage to their listeners and readers to persevere in the face of great difficulty.

POETRY: THE GREAT ART

Yemenis reserve one of the highest places in their culture for poets, who have played a part in shaping the course of events. The words of the late poet Muhammad Mahmoud al-Zubairi (1910—1965) helped to fuel the republican spirit during the struggle against the royalists, and he continues to hold pride of place in modern Yemen.

Contemporary poetry blossomed in the 1970s, when poets of the new generation, who had not been part of the revolution, began to voice their opinions about the times and their dreams of the future.

Lively, witty poetizing is a popular form of entertainment, and Yemeni poets have perfected the art of spontaneous poetry. A poetry competition is a popular way to show off one's verbal talent and wit. At a wedding, the men from each family will often challenge one another with clever wordplay to entertain the guests. Satirical poetry known as

"My homeland you are a whisper from God that does not part my heart or tongue.

God created my heart from your soil and extracted my soul from your scents.

If the flame of the heart proclaimed, they would say it passed through a Yemenite blade."

—Muhammad Mahmoud al-Zubairi

Perhaps the most famous and influential of modern Yemeni poets, Muhammad Mahmoud al-Zubairi came to public attention during the lead-up to the 1948 uprising against Imam Yahya. He used words to fight for political change. His poems reached their zenith during the period between the 1948 rebellion and the 1962 rebellion.

Arabic calligraphy covers the sheets above an open-air market.

hija (HEE-ja) is also a favorite. One poet composes a verse and sends it to a second poet, who responds using the same meter and rhyme.

Tribal disputes are often settled by a genre of poetry called *zamil* (ZA-mil). A tribal poet is the spokesperson for the tribe; his two-line zamils are sung by tribal members while they march toward the other tribe. The opposing tribe will then respond with its own zamil.

ARABIC CALLIGRAPHY

Calligraphy is a beautiful form of writing, but more important to the Yemenis, it is an artistic expression of Islamic spirituality used to decorate books and mosques. Calligraphy is not just a case of writing the text; the design should be as full of emotion and ideas as the words themselves. The relation between the black letters and the white space around them produces a striking composition and conveys the true meaning of the written word.

By tradition, the pen used for calligraphy is made from reed or cane. Since calligraphy began when the Quran was first written, the pen is symbolic of the written word of God:

And your Lord is the most generous,
Who has taught by the pen,
Taught humanity what it did not know.

ARCHITECTURE

Oral tradition describes a splendid palace called Ghumdan near Sanaa at the beginning of the Christian period, around the time of the kingdoms of Saba and Himyar. According to legend, the twenty stories of the palace towered above their surroundings, and each of the four sides was of colored stone: white, black, green, and red. It was said that bronze lions guarded the entrance to the palace and roared when the winds blew. The alabaster roof was so thin that from indoors one could see birds flying over it.

Historians confirm that there was an impressive cathedral in Sanaa, built around the same time as the Ghumdan palace. This church, known as al-Qalis, was made of teak and plated with gold and silver.

The arrival of Islam gave a new impetus to building. Just as Christianity inspired the Europeans to build cathedrals, Islam sparked its followers to build places of worship. Mosques were erected wherever there was a settlement.

The Great Mosque of Sanaa, which was built in 630 CE, is a wonder. Much of the material used to build this magnificent mosque was taken from older structures such as the Ghumdan palace and possibly from Sabean temples. Christian decorative motifs such as pigeons, doves, and rosettes appear on the minarets and parts of beams. Its wooden ceiling is inlaid with inscriptions and rich decorations.

THE ART OF BUILDING

In Yemen, a man's house is his castle. Great pride is taken in building it. On completion, decorative calligraphic writing records the event on the exterior wall. The house styles in Yemen are unique, and regional variations have evolved over the centuries.

The reed houses in the Tihama villages are round or rectangular with a pointed thatched roof. There is a striking contrast between the simple exterior and the artistic interior. Colorful designs are painted over the entire ceiling, and the inside is decorated with beautifully carved wooden furniture. These reed houses look just like those found across the Red Sea in Africa.

"I had a legendary vision that I am capable, with literature alone, to undermine a thousand years of corruption, injustice and oppression."
—Muhammad Mahmoud al-Zubairi

In the coastal town of Hodeida, houses are built in the Red Sea style. These are multistoried, with Turkish windows and balconies, and they reflect the foreign influence on Yemeni building styles.

The distinctive *zabur* (ZAH-boor) architecture is common on the plateaus of the eastern and northern highlands. Here there is plenty of clay, but stone is scarce. To build a zabur house, horizontal layers of clay are placed one on top of the other, as though one were making a chocolate layer cake. The walls are then coated with mud. Parapets decorated with small arches adorn the roof edges.

Tall houses are also a favorite in Hadramawt. The town of Shibam is often called the Manhattan of the Desert because it has more than five hundred mud-brick skyscrapers, some of which are more than 100 feet (30 m) above street level. Many of the Hadramawt houses are built from mud that has been sun-dried and made into bricks. After the walls have been built, they are plastered smooth with brown earth or light lime plaster.

DESIGN AND DECORATION

An important part of Yemeni culture is the use of intricate, geometric patterns painted in various color combinations to decorate the houses. The same patterns and motifs that women use to decorate their bodies are painted on walls, windows, doors, and ceilings, or carved into plaster and wood. The designs include zigzag lines, dots, floral patterns, and date-palm motifs.

On some houses, the windows are the most decorative element. The *takhrim* (TAHK-rim) windows in Sanaa are well known. They look as though they are covered with lace because their alabaster panes are shaped into delicate patterns. The addition of colored glass makes them even more charming, a wonderful sight to behold.

Doors and windows displaying skilled carpentry work may be all that remain to remind the world of Yemeni Jews. There are many fine examples of the high-quality work of Jewish craftsmen before their exodus and possible genocide. In the south, in cities such as Taiz, and in the Tihama, the influence of Indian workmanship can be seen in elaborate door carvings.

SILVERSMITHING

Traditional jewelry made of silver and crafted to local design is popular with women in Yemen. Sometimes colorful coral, amber, agate, glass, or ceramics are combined with the silver to create eye-catching pieces. The markets of Sanaa and Taiz are full of glittering head ornaments, necklaces, earrings, bangles, belts, and finger and nose rings. Finely crafted amulets, such as charm cases containing verses of the Quran, became popular after the arrival of Islam.

Yemeni Jews were renowned for their mastery in crafting jewelry. When they emigrated from Yemen in 1949 and 1950, Yemen ran the risk of losing one of its most profitable crafts, so it was decreed that any Jewish silversmith who planned to leave had to impart his skills to the Yemeni jewelers who remained.

CRAFTING WEAPONS

Weapon making is one of the most valued crafts in Yemen. The distinctive curved dagger known as the jambiya is worn on a special belt by Yemeni men. Its design varies according to the region, the tribe, and the social standing of the owner.

The tribesman's dagger is called an *asib* (as-EEB), and it has a bone or wooden handle. It is kept in a leather sheath and secured by a cloth belt. The asib is worn in the middle of the body, a sign of a free tribal warrior.

The elite qadis and sayyids wear a dagger known as a *thuma* (THU-ma), which has a slender curve and an ornate silver handle. They are kept in embroidered or carved wooden scabbards.

Well-crafted jambiyas are highly prized in Yemen.

In the past, Yemen was renowned throughout the world for making high-quality steel blades. Today, many of the blades are imported from Japan or Pakistan. The hilt, or handle, determines the value of the jambiya, and its carving is a marvel of craftsmanship. The most precious jambiyas are those made of African rhinoceros horn, which takes on a rich luster with age. Once carved, the hilts are embellished with silver, and coins are frequently mounted on them.

DANCE

Yemen has a long-standing and varied dance tradition. Each community has its own unique style of dance. There are dances that are intensely dynamic and those that are more subdued. Some are light and airy, while others involve a lot of hopping about.

One of the liveliest dances is the *bara* (ba-RAH). Each tribe has its own bara, which is characterized by the number of dancers, the way they command their daggers, the steps, and the music. Only men perform the bara, and always outdoors. It is danced during cooperative work projects, to welcome visitors, on festive occasions and national holidays, or simply when there is enough space to dance and people are in the mood.

In the northern highlands near Sanaa, as many as twenty men might dance the bara to the beat of drums. Arranged in a horseshoe, the men watch the leader, an accomplished dancer, who stands in the middle and signals a change of step. The men start moving slowly, but the pace soon builds to a feverish tempo, with complicated whirling and intricate steps. Daggers carried in the right hand are used to "cut the air." A great deal of skill is required to coordinate arms and legs so that nobody gets hurt.

Lub (li-BAH) is popular in parts of the highlands. The word *lub* means "to play," and as the name suggests, this dance is performed solely for entertainment. It is usually accompanied by love songs. A lub is often danced in pairs, and the partners are good friends or relatives. Sometimes men and women dance together, but only in the privacy of the family home.

MUSIC

There is a rich variety of music in Yemen. In the cities, people enjoy the soothing sounds of the oud, a short lute that resembles a guitar. It often accompanies the lovely voices of solo singers. Along the Red Sea coast, musicians use it to play lively rhythms.

Besides the oud, many other instruments are used to produce the stirring sounds of Yemeni music. The *simsimiya* (sim-sim-i-yah), a five-string lyre, is popular in the Tihama, along with cymbals and the violin. There are also reed windpipes, which make high-pitched buzzing sounds, as well as a variety of drums. In the highlands, musicians beat the drums with their hands and often also sing. Ahmad Fathi, born in Hodeida in the 1950s, is a famous Yemeni lute player.

Singing is a popular pastime for Yemenis, and there are many songs for them to choose from: religious songs, poetry chants, romantic ballads, and more. In the past, military songs were very popular, particularly during the revolutionary 1960s. Iskander Thabit from Aden, whose tunes carried many political statements, is practically a legend in Yemen. Today, the younger generation enjoys singing modern Arabic-language pop songs.

There are many popular Yemeni singers. Unfortunately, many Yemeni musicians have only been able to share their music from exile. Al-Yaman, a co-ed band based in the Czech Republic, blends modern styles with traditional Yemeni folk music to create performances that can be found on YouTube, among other sites.

The oud is a popular instrument in both Yemen and across the Arab world.

THE BANSKY OF YEMEN

Murad Subay, the street artist sometimes referred to as "The Banksy of Yemen," is one of many Yemeni artists working within the war zone, using their talent and their intelligence to try to shape the war for their fellow civilians. The pain of their shared suffering, and the underlying problem of war itself, is fodder for these artists.

Subay himself says his topic and theme is the war. "It is three letters only: W-A-R." His intention and goal is to tell his fellow Yemenis, the faction leaders, and the world of the catastrophe of Yemen's conflict. "It is just to show the ugliness of war—this is what happens by war. This is my way to protest against the injustice of war and for peace."

INTERNET LINKS

http://al-bab.com/commentary-yemeni-traditional-architecture
This article examines traditional Yemeni architecture.

https://www.aljazeera.com/indepth/features/2017/02/yemen-art -love-bombs-bans-170213090154650.html
This article describes the work of Murad Subay, known as "the Bansky of Yemen."

https://www.almadaniyamag.com/english/2017/11/30/muhammad -mahmoud-al-zubairi-the-conscience-of-yemen
This article discusses one of Yemen's most admired poets, Muhammad Mahmoud al-Zubairi.

LEISURE

Yemenis gather during the weekly market at Manakha.

11

TRADITIONALLY, DAILY LIFE IN Yemen involved plenty of social interaction. Trips to the mosque or the market involved greeting acquaintances, friends, and neighbors, and exchanging news and gossip. Of course, many relationships and leisure activities have been disrupted by the current civil war. Family remains an integral part of Yemeni culture, however, with entertainment and leisure time revolving largely around time spent with family members.

YEMENI GAMES

Yemeni children spend much of their time within the family and neighborhood, either helping with the household chores or playing with friends. When they have free time to play, older girls and boys usually have a younger brother or sister at their elbow. Boys tend to be more visible than girls. They are often seen huddling over dominoes or a board game, such as backgammon, in the street or the marketplace.

Girls usually play closer to the home, and their leisure activities are often connected with home concerns and the Yemeni love of poetry.

"My God ...
I will confess now
   I cheated the
      sparrows,
That I satirized the
      gardens,
I quarreled with the
      sun,
I made to the sea
      alone,
And waited out the
      beautiful time.
Nevertheless I get
      nothing but the
      waste."

—Dr. Abdulaziz al-Maqaleh

CAMEL RACING

A traditional sport in eastern Yemen is camel racing. The governorate of al-Mahrah is known for its well-bred camels that can run very fast because they are slender and extremely flexible. To deter camel thieves, the tribes who breed these prized beasts brand them with various signs. A good camel can cost 150,000 rials ($600).

In the afternoon, while their mothers are out visiting neighbors, some girls might play with dolls, while others make up their own games. They might sing, dance, and chant poetry. Sometimes the girls pick a theme, perhaps beauty or cooking, and hold poetry competitions among themselves.

Some traditional Yemeni children's games go back to ancient times and have been passed from one generation to the next. Unfortunately, few children play these games anymore. Other games and sports, such as soccer, have replaced them.

SPORTS

Soccer is a favorite pastime in Yemen. Children always seem to be kicking a ball around, whether they live in a small village or a city. If soccer balls are not available, there is always a plastic bottle or a homemade rag ball that will suffice.

Sports are played on a part-time basis. Even before the war, there were very few professional athletes who could compete internationally. In 1992, Yemen participated as a unified nation for the first time at the Olympic Games, in Barcelona, Spain. Yemen has competed in seven Olympic Games altogether, but no participant has won a medal yet.

WAR GAMES

Games have always reflected the cultures that created them and the times in which they came into existence. The old English game "Ring Around the Rosie," for example, notoriously had its start during the decades of the Black Plague. Similar bad times have created a new game in Yemen. It has been reported that Yemeni children now play a game they call "One, Two, Three, Airstrike," in which, as in "Ring Around the Rosie," the children all fling themselves to the ground, imitating the dead, the dying, and those attempting to escape the strike.

PUBLIC BATHHOUSES

A Yemeni proverb says, "The whole delight of this world lies in the hot bath." Public bathhouses are called *hammams*, and both men and women use them, although on different days. Bathhouses provide an important social activity for both men and women, a place to meet their friends and enjoy each other's company. They are also a favorite place for a bride and a groom to socialize separately with friends and relatives before a wedding.

A typical bathhouse is made up of three interconnecting rooms: the hot room, the warm room, and the cool room. The hot or steam room is normally built with a dome decorated with small glass windows that allow light to filter in. It usually has marble seating areas where the bathers can lie or sit. Once the bathers have had enough heat in the hot room, they proceed to wash themselves in the warm room. Sometimes they might ask a friend to help them. This is a great act of friendship. Finally they enter the cool room to relax, get dressed, and perhaps rehydrate their bodies by having a refreshing cup of tea. Some may even use the cool room to catch a nap after a massage. After the bath, the bathers will say to each other, "Hammam alhana," (HA-mahm ul-HA-na), which means "A pleasant bath," to which the polite reply is the same Arabic expression.

MEN'S SOCIAL GROUPS AND QAT PARTIES

The afternoons are quiet in many towns because both men and women often attend qat parties, which may last for as long as four hours. The parties take

The Honest Person and the Thief (a traditional game for boys)
Participants: five or more
Equipment: one matchbox (in early days, this game was played with a squared-off bone)
The players sit in a circle and take turns throwing a matchbox into the center. If the matchbox stands on its end, the thrower becomes "king." If it lands on one of the striking surfaces, the thrower becomes either "minister" or "soldier," based on markings made on the box or an agreement beforehand. If the box lands on one of the broad sides, the thrower is declared "honest" or "a thief" (again based on markings made beforehand). The thief receives a "sentence" that is decided by the minister, supervised by the soldier, and agreed to by the king. The sentence might consist of doing sit-ups or performing a service, such as making tea for the other players. Outrageous sentences are discouraged by the fact that any of the players could be the thief in the next game.

O Hillcock, O Hillcock (a traditional game for girls)
Participants: any number
Equipment: none
Two lines of girls stand facing each other, stamping their feet to the rhythm of a song. Each team selects a girl who has a talent for spontaneous poetry. A theme is chosen, the first poet comes up with a verse around the theme, and then her team chants her words. The second poet retorts, and the game continues until one of the girls succeeds in silencing the other.

place in the mafraj of a house, and everyone takes turns hosting them. The custom is to bring your own qat. Information about where the gathering will take place on a particular day is exchanged in the market or at the mosque.

Since verbal banter and jokes are important parts of Yemen's popular culture, the afternoon parties usually begin with the exchange of good-natured insults and jokes. Afterward, weighty subjects such as politics, business, religion, and the economy might be discussed in smaller groups or in pairs. Important business decisions are sometimes made at these gatherings. Quite often poetry is composed and recited. On a special occasion, there might be dancing, music, and singing. But there is usually some quiet time at the end of the gathering for enjoying the view or simply for meditation.

Chewing qat is an expensive habit. It is possible to tell how well-off a man is by the quality and quantity of the qat he chews.

WOMEN'S SOCIAL GROUPS

Yemeni women are not as restricted in public life as women in many other more conservative countries, such as Saudi Arabia. Even so, most of their activities take place within their homes or neighborhood.

In the afternoon, many women attend neighborhood gatherings. In cities such as Sanaa before the war, women would put on their best clothes, makeup, and jewelry to attend *tafritah* (ta-FREE-tah) circles. Conflict has slowed down or stopped many of these gatherings.

The tafritah takes place in the mafraj of one of the women's houses. The hostess passes around glasses of sweet tea and bowls of raisins, popcorn, or nuts to nibble on. A few of the women may chew qat. These gatherings offer women a chance to relax, exchange news, and discuss family issues with other women of the neighborhood. They also may listen to music and dance. From time to time, some of the older women might tell stories.

"If you give people nuts, you'll get shells thrown at you." —Yemeni proverb

INTERNET LINKS

https://balneorient.hypotheses.org/3158
This online exhibition shows photographs of Yemeni bathhouses.

https://www.theguardian.com/global-development-professionals -network/2015/nov/09/yemen-the-children-have-a-game-called -airstrike-in-which-they-fall-to-the-ground
This article describes daily life—and the new game children play—in Yemen during the civil war.

https://www.smithsonianmag.com/travel/the-sport-of-camel -jumping-54958431
This *Smithsonian* magazine article provides information on an interesting sport involving camels in Yemen.

FESTIVALS

Yemeni Muslims read the Quran during
the month of Ramadan.

YEMEN HAS SEVERAL RELIGIOUS AND
secular holidays that bring its
people together at certain times of
the year. The religious holidays focus on
Islamic holy days and celebrations, as
well as commemorative events. Secular
holidays are more often focused either
on political landmarks, like Yemen's
unification, or on features of the
agricultural year, including harvests.

12

"After three years of war, with overcrowded hospitals and skyrocketing prices, the people are not hopeful they will have a blessed Ramadan."
—Rudaw Media Network

RELIGIOUS EVENTS

Friday is a day of public prayer and the official day of worship and rest, when government offices are closed. Every Friday, observant Muslim men in Yemen try to offer their midday communal prayers in the mosque, where a religious leader delivers a special sermon.

The prophet Muhammad's birthday is honored by the majority of Yemenis. This is a quiet day that reminds worshippers of their Islamic faith and duties. At home, parents might read stories about Muhammad to their children.

Like Muslims in other countries, some Yemenis also honor Muhammad's death. On this day, they remember his ascension to heaven. In some areas, such as Sanaa, men and children spend the day visiting their female relatives.

RAMADAN

Ramadan is the ninth and most sacred month of the Islamic calendar. On the twenty-ninth day of the eighth month, Yemeni Muslims look toward the western horizon for the new moon. If it can be seen, Ramadan begins with the sunset. If not, Ramadan will begin the next day. The month is set aside for fasting, to commemorate Allah's revelations to Muhammad.

Muslims fast because Allah has commanded them to do so. Muslims also fast to enrich their spiritual life. They believe that a fast heightens spiritual awareness and brings one closer to God. Those who are ill or on a journey during the month of Ramadan do not fast but should later make up for the days lost. Very young children, pregnant women, and others with strong physical grounds for avoiding fasting conditions are also considered blameless if they refrain.

During Ramadan, a drummer wanders through the streets in the early hours of the morning before sunrise to wake the neighborhood by beating his drum or chanting in a loud voice. Yemenis rise, eat a small meal, and then fast for the rest of the day. During the daylight fast, neither beverages nor food will be consumed.

Iftan, the biggest meal of the day, is consumed after a cannon sounds at sunset. There is a special diet for this meal, which includes many nutritious foods such as soup, meat or cheese, fresh fruit juices, milk, dates, and figs. Sweets are eaten more than usual to give the body energy and are offered to friends and relatives who visit in the evening. Children often carry a colorful lantern with a candle inside when making their rounds of visits.

Ramadan is largely a nighttime-based celebration. Many Yemenis only wake near the time of noon prayers, having spent much of the night at family parties and in street celebrations. In the second half of Ramadan, it is a tradition for children to march around the neighborhood singing songs. They stop at houses to collect nuts, sweets, and donations.

The ongoing civil war has made Ramadan much more difficult for Yemenis. The luxurious dishes of Iftan, the sweets and drinks, are hard to find. The streets are not reliably safe. But there is also a feeling of passionate commitment on the part of resident Yemenis. This is their land, these are their traditions, and this is their own unique way of celebrating Islam's common heritage of Ramadan.

FEAST DAYS

The appearance of the new moon signals the end of Ramadan. At last, fasting is over, and it is time to celebrate Eid al-Fitr, the breaking of the fast. Often abbreviated to Eid, this festival is a time to give thanks to Allah. For many Muslims, Eid is also a time to give charity to the poor. It is an official public holiday, with no school or work for at least four days.

During Eid, children dress in special clothes bought to be worn only on these days. After breakfast, there are congregational prayers in the mosques, and relatives are visited. Children are then given some money and candies, and everyone eats a hearty lunch.

Eid al-Adha, or Feast of the Sacrifice, is another holiday. It starts on the tenth day of the month of the pilgrimage and is the highlight for those who have made the hajj. This holiday commemorates the obedient willingness of Ibrahim (Abraham in the Old Testament) to sacrifice his son to Allah. Many families sacrifice a lamb, which symbolizes giving oneself to God.

Yemeni boys carry sheep through the streets of Sanaa in preparation for the Eid al-Adha feast.

NONRELIGIOUS HOLIDAYS

Even after unification, Yemenis still observes some of the public holidays celebrated by the two earlier Yemens. The extent of the celebrations on these holidays depends on the region.

Revolution Day is celebrated in the south on October 14. This commemorates the day that the National Liberation Front (NLF) launched a revolution against British rule in South Yemen. The final withdrawal of the British and the subsequent formation of an independent state is celebrated on November 30 as Independence Day.

Northern Yemenis celebrate their Revolution Day on September 26, the day a group of military officers led by Colonel Abdullah Sallal overthrew the ruling imam in North Yemen and established the YAR.

Labor Day recognizes the contributions of Yemeni workers to the country's economic development.

The pomegranate holds a special place in the Middle East. A symbol of fortune and fertility, this fruit grows well even with comparatively little water. The plant, a small tree or medium-sized shrub, has dark, glossy leaves shaped like those of laurel or bay. The flowers are brilliant orange, shaped like a dancer's tutu with golden stamen and pistil. They leave behind the fruit hip, which over time expands to offer sweet-tart fruits loaded with individual seed cells, each bursting with juice. Pomegranate seeds and pomegranate juice are used in many Middle Eastern dishes. Pomegranate "molasses," a thickened version of the juice, is sweet, tart, and syrupy.

NATIONAL UNITY

The most significant modern event in Yemen was the end of national division and the establishment of the Republic of Yemen. For this reason, the Day of National Unity, celebrated on May 22, is the most important secular holiday for Yemenis. When not threatened by civil conflict, the day is honored with parades, traditional dancing and music, and sports events such as camel races and soccer games.

FARM FESTIVALS

Long ago, the Yemenis used astronomy as a guide to mark the seasons for planting. One of the most important stars in Yemeni tradition, Sirius, the Dog Star, is the brightest in the sky. In July, the dawn rising of this star signals the arrival of the late summer rains that have been, and still are, so important to farmers for irrigation purposes. Planting, harvesting, and the two rain periods remain a time of great rejoicing.

In some regions, ancient traditions are kept alive. Every September, Yemenis flock to the area of al-Jawf in al-Mahrah governorate, which borders Oman, to see the fall festival. The event is reminiscent of an ancient festival of that region that celebrated the end of the first monsoon rains.

Farmers share in the bounty of nature by enjoying themselves. During the festival, there is folk dancing and music, as well as sporting events such as camel races and tugs-of-war. Festival celebrations usually conclude with a public banquet.

GETTING MARRIED

A Muslim wedding in Yemen is a joyful occasion and is often celebrated over a number of days. The marriage ceremony consists of signing a contract in the presence of the qadi, an Islamic scholar of the law, who will recite the first sura of the Quran. The groom's father then throws a handful of raisins on the ground, symbolizing a happy future for the couple. Everyone present tries to gather as many raisins as he or she can.

Weddings in Sanaa are usually celebrated in a big way. The butchers arrive early in the morning to prepare meat for the feast. If the family can afford it, several sheep and even a calf will be bought for the meal.

When the groom arrives for the meal, he is accompanied by dancing and singing men. The bride arrives a little later with her father. It is customary for the women of the neighborhood to climb onto the roof of the house, where they welcome the newlyweds with high-pitched singing.

"If the time has passed, there is no point in preparing."
—Yemeni proverb

INTERNET LINKS

https://www.aljazeera.com/indepth/features/2017/06/recollection -yemen-ramadan-spirit-170606112356122.html
This article focuses on Ramadan and how it is celebrated in Yemen during the civil war.

https://nationalyemen.com/2014/06/29/ramadans-customs-and -traditions-vanish-with-life-development
This article examines changing religious customs and traditions in Yemen.

http://saudigazette.com.sa/article/11800/Yemeni-traditions -during-Ramadan
This article examines the particularly Yemeni way of celebrating Ramadan.

FOOD

Spices and grains are arrayed for sale at a Yemeni market.

13

THE YEMENI CULTURE PLACES enormous importance on hospitality and generosity— as do many Arab cultures.

"He who eats well is able to face an army."
—Yemeni proverb

Food and refreshment are very much a part of this ritual behavior. Yemenis are not only generous with their food—they are artistic, offering the best. The cook creates for family, friends, and strangers, always trying to present not just subsistence but a little slice of paradise.

Yemeni cooking is colored by its centuries at the heart of the great spice trade and the caravans that flowed from Europe, through India, and on to China and Southeast Asia. Yemeni cooks draw on a palette of flavors, scents, colors, and cooking methods that is unsurpassed in its scope.

CUISINE

The Yemeni diet is simple and nourishing, using locally grown grains such as sorghum, millet, and corn, along with flour made from legumes. Fruit and vegetables vary across the country, depending on how fertile the land is. Sometimes Yemenis eat chicken and mutton, particularly if there is a special occasion, such as when a child is born, when guests come to dinner, or when a person is ill and is believed to need richer nourishment. No pork is eaten in this Muslim culture.

KITCHENS

Some traditional kitchens in Yemen can be dark because the windows are kept closed to prevent dust from getting into the food. When the cooking fires are lit, the kitchens can become unbearably hot.

Many kitchens in Yemen have at least one *tannur* (TANN-ur), a cylindrical clay oven. These tannurs fall within the same cooking tradition as Indian or Pakistani tandoors. Tannurs come in all sizes, and women say there is a real knack to breaking in the cook for tannur baking. What they mean is that it takes a while to get accustomed to getting the heat of the tannur just right so that one can slap the bread onto the insides of the oven. Young girls get lots of practice on smaller tannurs before they progress to larger ones.

"Work like an
ant and you'll
eat sugar."
—Yemeni proverb

Yemenis are fiercely proud of locally produced foodstuffs, known as baladi *(BAHL-a-di), which means "of the country." Such products are believed to be superior in quality to foreign foods. Yemenis purchase them whenever they are available.*

Locally produced honey is a delicacy that is in great demand. It is an essential ingredient in many traditional recipes. Even a slight variation from the local flavor is an indication that the honey is impure. Honey is also a status symbol and is frequently given as a gift. Some of the most expensive honey in the world comes from the Hadramawt region.

There is a little hole at the bottom of the tannur where bits of fuel, such as charcoal or wood, are put in. When food needs to be grilled or broiled, a grate can be placed over the top opening, and the food is placed on it.

Besides the tannur, most kitchens are equipped with charcoal braziers to keep coffeepots warm. Many urban homes have gas stoves.

The conventional Yemeni refrigerator consists of an alcove in the wall with wooden doors. A big jar of water sits inside. The outside wall has holes so that when the wind blows through them, evaporation cools the water in the jar and keeps the food fresh. Sometimes when the women are bored, they will peer through the holes to see what is happening in the streets.

For washing up, there is a kitchen sink, which is a shallow trough on a ledge leading to an outside drain. If the kitchen does not have a tap, water will be collected and stored in great earthenware jars.

Cookware is stored on shelves above the oven. There are aluminum saucepans, stone pots, and plenty of bread baskets. Spices and herbs hang in baskets on the walls. There are rolling pins for dough, pestles for crushing grains, and hand mills to grind corn or pepper. Scissors are used for just about everything—from cutting vegetables to removing the legs from a chicken.

COOKING

Women often prepare food on trays while kneeling on the floor. To make bread, dough is stretched across a stone and then slapped against the walls of the piping hot tannur. While bread is baking, a broth or a stew might be simmering in a clay pot. Meanwhile, someone will prepare *hilbah* (HUHL-bah), a dip for bread. Hilbah is uncommon in rural areas but is a favorite in the cities. Other popular dips and sauces for bread include tangy tomato, garlic, and red pepper sauces that are mixed by hand or in an electric blender.

MEALS

For religious Yemenis, the day starts early with the dawn prayer. After prayer, some Yemenis have something light, such as tea and a piece of bread. Others

A Yemeni family shares a meal by candlelight.

wait until 8 a.m. to eat breakfast. This typically consists of scrambled eggs or cooked beans, along with bread or porridge.

Lunch is the biggest meal of the day in Yemen. If male guests are invited, the men eat first, and then the women eat. Otherwise the whole family eats together. Lunch in Sanaa might start with a few radishes dipped in a fenugreek sauce to whet the appetite. Then the wheat or sorghum porridge follows, or a cold pancake with a hint of mint or thyme, to satisfy hunger pangs.

A vegetable stew, potatoes, beans, and plenty of bread and hilbah ensure that even the heartiest appetite is fully satisfied. Unlike Western meals, where meat is served during the main course, in Yemen meat is always served at the end of a meal.

For those with a sweet tooth, dessert could be fresh fruit, a caramel pudding, or a hot, flaky pastry with honey. After the meal, tea and coffee are served in another room, where people can relax, and the men can chew qat.

For most people, supper is a simple, light meal that the women prepare after the sunset prayer. Supper often consists of the day's leftovers, perhaps chicken or eggs with tomatoes, bread, and water.

TABLE MANNERS

It is a Yemeni custom to share food generously. When offered food, one should accept graciously so that the host is not offended. Refusing food is understood to mean one of three things: the guest feels the host cannot really afford to be so generous; the food is unclean or not prepared properly; or the guest does not like the host. Turning down food, therefore, is a social blunder and an insult to the host.

Yemenis eat their meals while sitting on the floor rather than at a table. Before they eat, they wash their hands. Yemenis eat from communal dishes, taking the food from the part closest to them. Meat and vegetables are scooped up with bits of bread or with the right hand.

The most common bean used in Yemeni cuisine is the broad bean, also known as the fava, or, in Arabic, *ful* (FOOL). This is one of the varieties of bean native to Eurasia, and it has been one of the foundations of Middle Eastern cooking since prehistory.

A Yemeni woman shapes dough into round loaves.

FAVORITES

Every community has its favorite fare. City folk enjoy fruit, honey, vegetable stews, salads, and rice. Along the coast, people eat fish. The tribal people love their local porridges, which are highly nutritious.

Bread is to Yemenis what pasta is to Italians. Every day the women of the household will bake enough bread for breakfast, lunch, and dinner. There are many types of breads, and most are made from local grains. *Khubz tawwa* (KU-butz tah-WAH) is ordinary bread that is fried at home, and *lahuh* (LAH-huh) is a festive pancake made from sorghum. In the cities, modern bakeries sell oblong roti loaves. The word "roti" was introduced a long time ago by Indians who traded in the port of Aden.

The national urban dish is *saltah* (SAHL-tah), which means "soup." The favorites are lamb or thick lentil soup with vegetables such as beans. Sometimes a refreshing green yogurt soup called *shafut* (SHA-fuht), made with sour milk mixed with chili, beans, and herbs, is poured over bits of bread and eaten in the afternoon.

A typical dessert is *bint al-sahn* (bint al-SA-han), a sweet bread made from eggs. This is dipped in a mixture of butter and honey.

The world-famous Yemeni coffee from the port of Mocha is not as commonly drunk as tea because it is more expensive. People also drink a flavorful brew known as *qishr* (KU-shir). The drink is made from ground coffee husks and ginger. For those who prefer a stronger coffee, there is *bunn* (BUN), a traditional coffee made straight from the beans. For Yemenis, the perfect end to a meal is tea in small glasses, usually very sweet, and sometimes flavored with cardamom or mint.

INTERNET LINKS

https://www.thenational.ae/lifestyle/food/food-trails-the-rich -history-of-yemeni-cuisine-1.157071
This article examines the rich history of Yemeni cuisine.

https://www.pbs.org/newshour/show/how-food-became-a-weapon -of-war-in-yemen
This article explores how food has become a "weapon of war" during the Yemeni civil war.

https://www.star2.com/food/recipes/2017/06/03/unique-yemeni -recipes-ramadan
This website offers a range of Yemeni recipes for Ramadan.

FUL (YEMENI SPICED BEANS)

This common dish made with broad beans comes in a million versions, with each cook creating dishes traditional to their family, or improvising from available ingredients.

2 pounds (1 kilogram) broad beans, soaked
   in warm water for at least one hour
2 onions, chopped coarsely
1 head garlic, peeled and crushed
1 15-ounce (444-milliliter) can of
   diced tomatoes
1 bell pepper, chopped
Salt to taste
Paprika or cayenne to taste
1 teaspoon minced chili or more,
   depending on spice preference
2 heaping tablespoons of turmeric
3 tablespoons of cumin

Place beans in a pot. Cover with water, and simmer at low heat until tender—between one to two hours—adding water as needed. Drain the beans, reserving the cooking water. Place beans in a colander and run under cool water until you can bear to handle the beans. Once you can handle the beans, strip the tough skins from the beans.

Next, fry your onion, garlic, and peppers in oil until soft. Add dried seasonings to the aromatic vegetables. Add tomatoes and cook until the flavors meld and the tomatoes are soft.

Place peeled beans, reserved water, and the pan of vegetables and spices in a single cooking pot with enough room left to simmer. Cook until the stew begins to thicken. Serve hot, with bread or grain. This keeps well, improving over the next few days. It is easy to reheat on the stovetop or in the microwave.

YEMENI CHICKEN AND POTATO

1 tablespoon oil

3—4 large potatoes sliced about ¾ inches (2 centimeters) thick.

8 chicken thighs

3 cups (705 mL) chicken broth or water

½ head of garlic

1 teaspoon cardamom

½ teaspoon minced fresh hot chili or black pepper to taste

1 pinch crushed saffron

½ teaspoon cinnamon

1 teaspoon cumin

1½ tablespoons cornstarch, plus water to make slurry

Lemon juice from 3 lemons

Lemon zest from ½ lemon or to taste

Fresh minced cilantro

Oil a deep baking pan. Place potatoes in a layer on the bottom of the pan. Layer the chicken on top of the potatoes. In a pot, combine the broth and seasonings up to the cornstarch. Bring to a lively simmer, and add cornstarch slurry—stir until the water thickens. Add more cornstarch slurry if needed to create a light gravy. Add lemon juice and ½ lemon zest. Pour over the chicken and potatoes, and cook in a moderate oven, basting often with the seasoned gravy. When the chicken is tender and the potatoes are cooked—about 30—45 minutes—remove from the oven and sprinkle with chopped fresh cilantro and fresh lemon zest. Serve with rice.

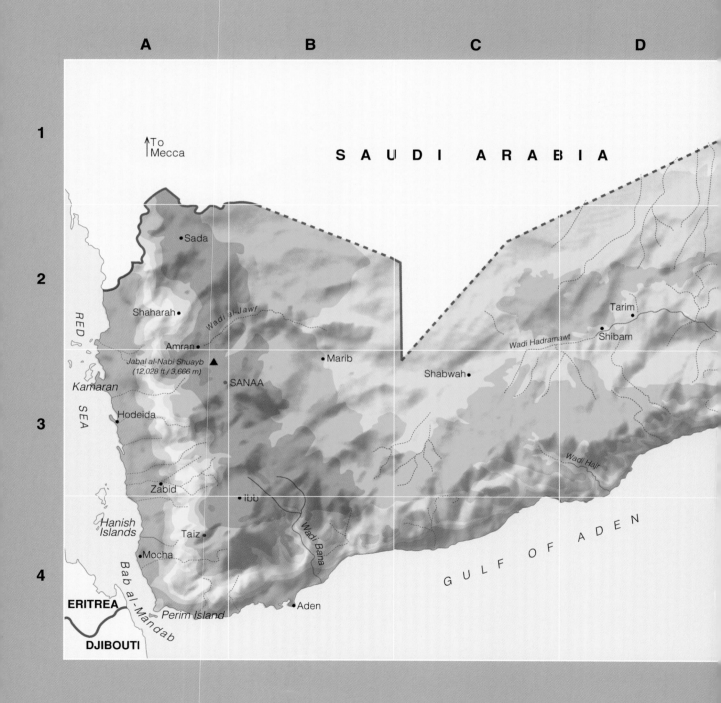

MAP OF YEMEN

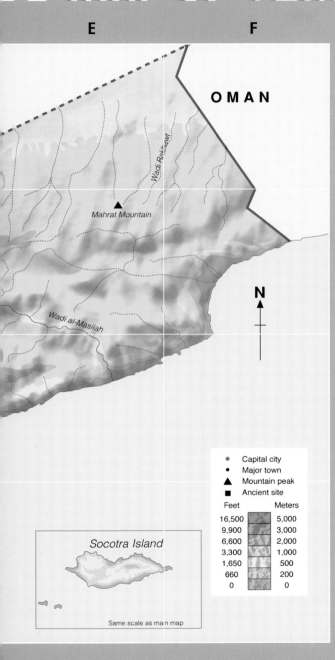

E   F

OMAN

Wadi Rakhawt

Mahrat Mountain

Wadi al-Masilah

N

Capital city
Major town
Mountain peak
Ancient site

Feet	Meters
16,500	5,000
9,900	3,000
6,600	2,000
3,300	1,000
1,650	500
660	200
0	0

Socotra Island

Same scale as main map

Aden, B3
Amran, A2

Bab al-Mandab, A4

Djibouti, A4

Eritrea, A4

Gulf of Aden, B4,
  C4, D3—D4

Hanish Islands,
  A3—A4
Hodeida, A3

Ibb, B3—B4

Jabal al-Nabi
  Shuayb
  Mountain, A3

Kamaran, A3

Mahrat Mountain,
  E2
Marib, B3
Mocha, A4

Oman, F1—F2

Perim Island, A4

Red Sea, A1—A3

Sada, A2
Sanaa, A3
Saudi Arabia, A1—
  A2, B1—B2, C1—
  C3, D1—D2, E1, F1
Shabwah, C2
Shaharah, A2
Shibam, D2
Socotra Island, E4,
  F4

Taiz, A4
Tarim, D2

Wadi al Jawf, A2,
  B2
Wadi al Masilah,
  E2—E3
Wadi Bana, B3—B4
Wadi Hadramawt,
  C2—C3, D2
Wadi Hajr, C3, D3
Wadi Rakhawt,
  E1—E2, F1

Zabid, A3

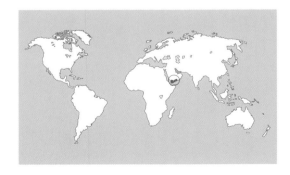

ECONOMIC YEMEN

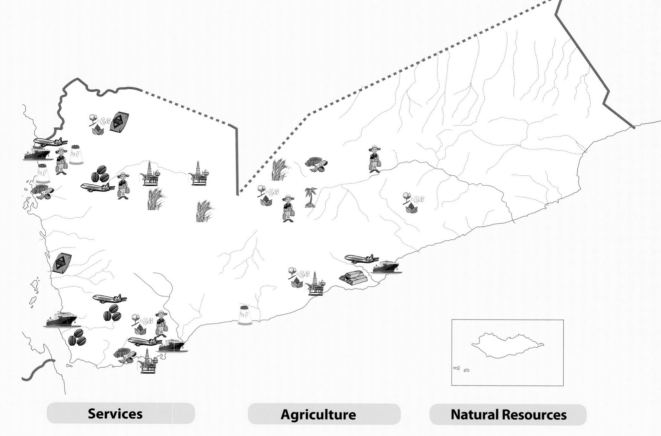

Services

 Airport

Port

 Tourism

Agriculture

Fruits

Coffee

Cotton

Date palm

Sesame

Tobacco

Wheat

Natural Resources

 Gold

Salt

Manufacturing

Cement

Petroleum refinery

ABOUT THE ECONOMY

OVERVIEW

Yemen is one of the poorest countries of the Arabian Peninsula. The discovery of oil boosted the country's sluggish economy, and between 2000 and 2007, the country reported growth of up to 4 percent per year. In 2008, however, growth fell to 3 percent. This was a result of falling oil prices and the global economic slowdown, which directly affected the demand for oil. To strengthen its economy, Yemen established strategies to diversify its earnings by attracting more foreign investment and supporting its nonoil sectors. In August 2014, the IMF approved a $570 million Extended Credit Facility (loan) for Yemen. However, the civil conflict that began that year derailed many of those efforts, and the economic decline has intensified. The country's foreign reserves were decimated, and there is little in the way of programs for the needy, or even access to food or medical equipment due to the conflict on the ground.

GROSS DOMESTIC PRODUCT (GDP)

$25.67 billion (2017 est.)

GDP PER CAPITA

$990 (2017 est.)

CURRENCY

Yemeni rial (YER)
$1 = 250 YER (2018 est.)

GROWTH RATE

—2 percent (2017 est.)

LABOR FORCE

7.425 million (2017 est.)

MAIN EXPORTS

Crude oil, coffee, dried and salted fish, liquefied natural gas

MAIN IMPORTS

Food and live animals, machinery and equipment, chemicals

MAIN TRADE PARTNERS

China, India, Thailand, United Arab Emirates, Saudi Arabia, Turkey, Egypt, Oman, Belarus, Brazil

AGRICULTURAL PRODUCTS

Grain, fruits, vegetables, pulses, qat, coffee, cotton, dairy products, livestock (sheep, goats, cattle, camels), poultry, fish

NATURAL RESOURCES

Petroleum; fish; rock salt; marble; small deposits of coal, gold, lead, nickel, and copper; fertile soil in the west

CULTURAL YEMEN

Sanaa

Sanaa was declared a UNESCO World Heritage site by the United Nations in 1986. It is a premedieval city, fortified by ancient clay walls, containing a host of ancient buildings, including mosques, houses, and public baths. A unique feature of the houses in the old city is that many of them resemble intricately decorated skyscrapers—they are flat-roofed towers several stories in height. Built more than seven hundred years ago, Bab al-Yaman, or Yemen Gate, is a legendary entry point through the old city walls. Sanaa is also home to the awe-inspiring Jami al-Kabir, the Great Mosque, which was built in the seventh century CE and ranks among the oldest mosques in the Islamic world. Sanaa is no longer the seat of the internationally recognized government of Yemen, which was moved to Aden in 2015.

Souk al-Milh

Souk al-Milh, the Salt Market, is Sanaa's main souk. The best time to visit is in the early morning or the early evening, when it is a hive of activity, bursting with shoppers. There is a wide variety of goods on sale, such as spices, vegetables, corn, qat, pottery, raisins, copper, woodwork, and clothing.

Shibam

Shibam is a sixteenth-century city surrounded by a fortified wall. Nicknamed the Manhattan of the Desert because of its unique towerlike houses that rise out of the cliff, Shibam was declared an UNESCO World Heritage site in 1982. It is believed that these distinct tower houses were built as a form of protection against bedouin attacks.

Mocha

Mocha is a port city situated on the coast of the Red Sea. During the fifteenth to seventeenth centuries, it was well known for being the marketplace for coffee. Merchants from all over Europe came to Mocha to trade. The term "mocha coffee" is derived from this ancient port. Even today, mocha coffee beans are appreciated the world over for their distinctive flavors.

Beit al-Faqih

Beit al-Faqih is located 37 miles (60 km) from Hodeida. It was one of the largest and busiest commercial centers for the coffee trade during the seventeenth and eighteenth centuries. It also served as an important storage station for Yemen's coffee crop. The men of this ancient city are well known for wearing unusual short skirts known as *al-lahafat*.

Aden

Aden has been an urban coastal settlement since ancient times. The port's enviable position on the most important sea route between India and Europe brought it to the attention of many ancient rulers who desired to possess it. Legend has it that Cain and Abel founded Aden. The internationally recognized government of Yemen moved its capital to Aden from Sanaa in 2015.

Zabid

Zabid is famous for being the seat of Islamic learning and the site of an important early Islamic seminary. Continuing the tradition, today the city and its surrounding areas are home to more than eighty madrassas, or Muslim schools. It was the capital of the Banu Ziyad dynasty in the early ninth century CE.

Al-Djanad

Al-Djanad is a courtyard mosque located in a tiny village north of Taiz. It is believed to be the second mosque built in Yemen, making it one of the oldest mosques in the Muslim world, together with the Great Mosque in Sanaa. It was built in the lifetime of the prophet Muhammad.

Taiz

Taiz is a city dramatically situated in the highlands close to the famous port of Mocha on the Red Sea. Taiz is overlooked by the majestic Jabal Saber. Although it is a modern industrial city, many of its old white mosques and beautiful ancient quarters remain intact. The city is famous for its old citadel and the Governor's Palace, which sits high above the city center.

Socotra Island

Socotra is a picturesque island situated at the entrance of the Gulf of Aden in the Indian Ocean, approximately 220 miles (354 km) from the Yemeni mainland. The name of the island is believed to have derived from the Sanskrit phrase *dvipa sakhadara*, or "island of bliss." An island of outstanding natural beauty, Socotra has distinct species of flora including frankincense, myrrh, and dragon's blood tree.

Wadi Hadramawt

Wadi Hadramawt is the largest wadi in the Arabian Peninsula. The graves of many pre-Islamic prophets and saints can be found there. Wadi Hadramawt can be entered through the Rub al-Khali desert and Djol mountain plateau. It is a fertile oasis surrounded by date palms and majestic sandrock mountains. The cities of Shibam, Sayun, and Tarim are located within Wadi Hadramawt.

ABOUT THE CULTURE

OFFICIAL NAME
Republic of Yemen (Arabic: al-Yaman)

CAPITAL
Sanaa

POPULATION
28 million (2017 est.)

MAIN CITIES
Sanaa, Aden, Taiz, Hodeida

OFFICIAL LANGUAGE
Arabic

PORTS
Aden, Hodeida, Mocha

ADMINISTRATIVE DIVISIONS
22 governorates: Abyan, Aden, Ad Dali, al-Bayda, al-Hodeida, al-Jawf, al-Mahrah, al-Mahwit, Amanat al-Asimah (Sanaa city), Amran, Dhamar, Hadramawt, Hajjah, Ibb, Lahij, Marib, Raymah, Sada, Sanaa, Shabwah, Socotra, Taiz

LAND AREA
203,850 square miles (527,970 sq km)

NATIONAL FLAG
Three equal horizontal bands of red (top), white, and black; similar to the flag of Syria, which has two green stars in the white band, and of Iraq, which has an Arabic inscription centered in the white band; also similar to the flag of Egypt, which has a heraldic eagle centered in the white band

HIGHEST POINT
Jabal al-Nabi Shuayb, 12,028 feet (3,666 m)

NATIONAL EMBLEM
The eagle, a symbol of the strength and liberty of the nation

ETHNIC GROUPS
Predominantly Arab, but also Afro-Arab, South Asian, and European

MAJOR RELIGIONS
Muslim, both Shafi (Sunni) and Zaidi (Shia)

BIRTHRATE
28.4 births/1,000 population (2017 est.)

DEATH RATE
6 deaths/1,000 population (2017 est.)

LIFE EXPECTANCY
65.9 years (2017 est.)

TIMELINE

IN YEMEN	IN THE WORLD
1500s Ottomans absorb part of Yemen into their empire but are expelled in the 1600s.	**1776** The US Declaration of Independence is signed.
	1789–1799 The French Revolution.
1839 Aden comes under British rule.	
1869 Yemen serves as a major refueling port as the Suez Canal opens.	**1914** World War I begins.
1918 Ottoman Empire dissolves as North Yemen gains independence and is ruled by Imam Yahya ibn Mohammed.	**1939** World War II begins.
1962 Army officers seize power and set up the Yemen Arab Republic (YAR), sparking civil war between royalists and republicans.	**1945** The United States drops atomic bombs on Hiroshima and Nagasaki. World War II ends.
1967 South Yemen is formed; the country is later officially known as the People's Democratic Republic of Yemen (PDRY).	**1980** The Soviet invasion of Afghanistan begins.
1986 Thousands die in the south due to political rivalry. PDRY president Ali Nasser Muhammad flees the country and is later sentenced to death for treason. A new government is formed.	**1989** The Berlin Wall falls.
1990 Unified Republic of Yemen is proclaimed, with Ali Abdullah Saleh as president.	
1993 Coalition government is formed from the ruling parties of the former YAR and PDRY. Saleh declares a state of emergency. Northern forces take control of Aden in July.	**1997** Hong Kong is returned to China.
2002 Yemen expels foreign Islamic scholars.	**2001** Terrorists crash planes into New York, Washington, DC, and Pennsylvania.
2005 Fighting begins again between	**2003** The War in Iraq begins.

IN YEMEN	IN THE WORLD
government forces and supporters of the slain rebel cleric Hussein al-Houthi.	**2005** Hurricane Katrina devastates the Gulf Coast of the United States.
2006 President Saleh wins another term in the September elections.	
2007 Scores are killed or wounded in clashes between security forces and Houthi rebels in the north. Rebel leader Abdul-Malik al-Houthi accepts a cease-fire in June.	
2008 Clashes renew in January between security forces and rebels loyal to Abdul-Malik al-Houthi.	**2008** A global financial crisis begins in the United States, leading to what economists call the greatest economic downtown since the Great Depression in the 1930s.
2009 Yemen's parliament approves a two-year postponement of its legislative elections in an attempt to calm tensions between the governing party and the opposition over the fairness of elections.	
2011 Houthi Shia factionalists object to Saleh's administration and rebel. This is the first major step in the collapse of the Republic of Yemen. President Saleh agrees to resign and appoints Vice President Hadi to take his place until elections.	**2011** The Arab Spring, a broad collection of uprisings throughout Arab nations, begins.
2012 Abdrabbuh Mansur Hadi is sworn into office. Fighting continues.	
2014 The Houthis and the Hadi administration agree to a cease-fire in September.	
2016 The Houthis officially form a new government in Sanaa.	**2016** Citizens of the United Kingdom vote to leave the European Union.
2017 A cholera outbreak kills thousands. Former president Saleh is assassinated.	**2017** Donald Trump is sworn in as president of the United States.
2018 Civil conflict continues with severe food and medical equipment shortages.	**2018** The Winter Olympics take place in Pyeongchang, South Korea.

GLOSSARY

abaya
A loose black robe from head to toe; traditionally worn by Muslim women.

bara (ba-RAH)
Dance with variations in the steps and the number of dancers depending on the tribe.

Bedouin
Camel-breeding tribes who roam the deserts.

bunn (BUN)
Traditional strong coffee.

futa (FOO-ta)
Gathered calf-length skirt worn by men.

Hadith
The collection of the prophet Muhammad's sayings that supplements the Quran in guiding Muslims.

hammam alhana (HA-mahm ul-HA-na)
An Arabic expression meaning "a pleasant bath."

hija (HEE-ja)
Satirical poetry.

hijab
A headscarf worn by Muslim women to conceal the hair and neck.

insha Allah (EEN-sha Allah)
A social greeting that means "God willing."

lub (li-BAH)
A form of dance.

masjid (MAHS-jid)
A place of prayer and worship.

oud
Musical instrument similar to a lute.

qadis
Islamic scholars of law.

saltah (SAHL-tah)
A soup popular in the cities.

sharshaf (SHAHR-shahf)
Loose, black cloak worn by Yemeni women.

sheikh
A tribal leader.

sitara (SEE-tahr-a)
Brightly colored cloak worn by Yemeni women.

tafritah (ta-FREE-tah)
A women's gathering that usually takes place in the afternoon.

tannur (TANN-ur)
A cylindrical earthenware oven.

tarboosh
A round hat worn by Yemeni men.

wadi
A dry riverbed filled in rainy seasons.

zamil (ZA-mil)
A genre of tribal poetry.

FOR FURTHER INFORMATION

BOOKS

Gaston, E. L. *Justice and Security Dialogue in Yemen: Negotiating Local Sources of Conflict Amid National Transition*. Washington, DC: United States Institute of Peace, 2015.

Rabi, Uzi. *Yemen: Revolution, Civil War, and Unification*. New York: I. B. Tauris, 2015.

Sonneborn, Liz. *Yemen*. New York: Children's Press, 2015.

Wagner, Mark S. *Jews and Islamic Law in Early Twentieth-Century Yemen*. Bloomington: Indiana University Press, 2015.

FILMS

Ahmad, Safa al-, and Ghaith Abdul Ahad. *The Fight for Yemen*. PBS, 2015.

Ishaq, Sara. *The Mulberry House*. No Nation Films, 2013.

Salami, Khadija al-. *I Am Nojoom, Age 10 and Divorced*. Benji Films, 2014.

MUSIC

Jewish Music Research Centre at the Hebrew University of Jerusalem. *With Songs They Respond: The Diwan of the Jews from Central Yemen*. The Eight Note, 2018.

Junayd, Hamud al-. *Traditional Yemeni Songs*. Nimbus Records, 2015.

Various. *The Music of Islam, Vol. 11: Music of Yemen, Sanaa, Yemen*. Celestial Harmonies, 2011.

Zafa. *Funky Grooves of Yemen*. Blue Pie, 2007.

BIBLIOGRAPHY

BOOKS

Hamalainen, Pertti. *Yemen*. London, UK: Lonely Planet Travel Guides, 1999.

Hansen, Eric. *Motoring with Mohammed*. Boston: Houghton Mifflin, 1991.

Johnson-Davies, Denys. *Desert Fox Seif bin Ziyazan*. Cairo, Egypt: Hoopoe Books, 1996.

Khalidi, Marion. *Queen of Sheba*. London, UK: Hood-Hood Books, 1996.

Mackintosh-Smith, Tim. *Yemen: Travels in Dictionary Land*. London, UK: John Murray, 1997.

Serjeant, R. B., and Ronald Lewcock. *Sanaa: an Arabian Islamic City*. London, UK: Scorpion Communications and Publications, 1983.

WEBSITES

CIA World Factbook, https://www.cia.gov/library/publications/the-world-factbook/index.html.

Encyclopedia of the Nations, http://www.nationsencyclopedia.com.

Foreign and Commonwealth Office, https://www.fco.gov.uk.

NationMaster, http://www.nationmaster.com

The UN Refugee Agency, http://www.unhcr.org.

INDEX

INDEX